Chaplain CPE Library

Hold Me,

Help Me,

Heal Me

D1512084

A CONCERNED COMMUNICATIONS PUBLICATION

Hold Me, Help Me, Heal Me

Copyright ©1997 by Sandy Wyman Richert

Publisher: Russ L. Potter, II
Senior Editor: Bill Morelan • Editor: Pat Benton
Copy Editor: Mary Alice Hill • Cover: MOE studios

All international rights reserved. Except for brief quotations in reviews,
no part of this publication may be reproduced, stored, or transmitted in any form
or by any means (mechanical, electronic, photocopy, recording, etc.)
without expressed written permission from the publisher:
Concerned Communications • P.O.Box 1000, Siloam Springs, AR 72761
Scripture taken from the HOLY BIBLE, NEW INTERNATIONAL VERSION.
Copyright ©1973, 1978, 1984 International Bible Society
Used by permission of Zondervan Bible Publishers

ISBN#0-936785-94-2

Dedication

To my children,
Todd and Taryn:
You continually show me
that life is to be lived

Property of the U.S. Government
Department of Veterans Affairs
Chaplain Service
Please return to CPE Library

Property of the U.S. Government
Department of Veterans Affairs
Chaplain Service
Please return to CPE Library

Property of the U.S. Government
Department of Veterans Affairs
Chaplain Service
Please return to CPE Library

Property of the U.S. Government
Department of Veterans Affairs
Chaplain Service
Please return to CPE Library

Contents

Acknowledgments

To my parents, Lloyd and Donna Wyman:
It's obvious to say that I'm here because of you! Yet I'm truly
who I am because of you. Thank you for always believing in me,
and for supporting me even when it hurts. There's not enough
room on this page to express how I love you.

To my brother, Scott:
You've been so much more than a brother to me. I love you.
Please forgive me for not feeling that way when I was 12!

To my children, Todd and Taryn:
I love you more than my life. You teach me something new every day.
How lucky I am to be your mom.

To the memory of Trevor:
I will cling to the love we shared and the inspiration you were
until the day I can hold you again.

To my editor, Pat Horning Benton:
Your gifted and gracious pruning was indispensable. The fact that
you made it fun and painless was a bonus. Thank you.

To the Arroyo Grande church:
You will always be like family to me. Thank you for not being afraid
to walk through this valley with me.

To all who have shared their journeys and prayers with me:
Our rivers of tears have mixed as one. God bless you.

To my special "family" at It Is Written *television:*
What a privilege to work together in getting this Good News to
all the world, so our Lord can come and we can go home!
I love you all. Special thanks to Mark, Pauline, Manuel, Kelly,
Connie, Merrilou, Charles, Jennifer, and Matt.

To all of you I have not met yet, who are hurting and confused:
You are the reason this book exists. I will pray for God to draw
especially close to you right now.

Most importantly, to my ever-loving and merciful Heavenly Father:
How thankful I am that grace is undeserved! Come quickly Lord—
I long to see you face to face.

I am where I am today because of all of you. Thank you!

Preface

**"May the God of hope fill you with all joy
and peace as you trust in him. . ."**
—*Romans 15:13, NIV*

I'm sharing my journey with you because of two promises that I made:

To God, when I was just a child, that I wanted to live my life so that others would see Him clearly. I haven't always kept that promise—in fact I've fogged up the view many times. This book is meant to reveal a God who is forever for us and with us.

To my 7-year-old son, Trevor, who lay dying from a brain tumor, that others would learn of his struggle—and of his faith, courage, and inspiration.

To put this story in writing is the fulfillment of these promises, and I'm humbled by the prospect of what God will do. Many of you who are holding this book were among the hundreds who lifted Trevor and our family in prayer. My heart beats with gratitude to you. I want you to know that your prayers were and are being answered in ways that you'd never imagine.

I'm sharing an intense experience about the life and death of a child who loved Jesus, a child who had a brief time to spend loving with his family before the end. My story is not unique; many of you have laid a child—or another loved one—to rest, and my heart goes out to you right now.

I believe we can—and *must*—entrust all our pain and confusion to God. Recently I heard this one-sentence description of how we implore God: "We beat on His chest from within the circle of His arms." I've discovered that in our pain we are brought most intimately into fellowship with our heavenly Father.

I've divided this book into three sections. You might find it most useful to read the first in one sitting. It describes the sweet life and painful, yet powerful, death of Trevor. The rest of the book can be sampled one chapter at a time.

In the second section I share some of the profound realities that I've come to embrace. I've been helped so much by the shared experience and insights of many Christian authors. You'll find a substantial reading list at the end of the book. The final section offers suggestions to help you or another who is grieving. Many people want to help a friend or loved one who's experiencing loss, but they don't know what to do or say. Perhaps these chapters will provide insights about helping in a healing way.

You may sense throughout the story that Trevor's father and I are no longer together. I'll not assume what his journey has been, but I want to emphasize that he was deeply loved by Trevor and is an adoring father to his children.

I've not completed my journey; that will take a lifetime. But I invite you to join me in giving our brokenness, our confusion, our doubts, and our fears to Him. He will take our burdens and give us in return a peace that passes understanding.

I pray that as you turn these pages you'll discover that He passionately longs to hold you, help you, and heal you!

Expecting a blessing,

Sandy Wyman Richert

Foreword

There's something especially traumatic about the death of a child. When a parent or grandparent dies, the family loses its past—but when a child dies, the family loses its future.

When death draws near a child who has been ill, the child may fear the dark; he may fear to be alone; he may fear to die in pain. So it's time for the family to band together to assure the little person that he won't be alone. It's a time to affirm him, to let him know that he'll not needlessly suffer. It's a time to join him in trusting everything to Jesus.

Grandparents have a unique role to play in the terminal illness and death of a grandchild. They suffer a double whammy: feeling the pain and anxiety of a deeply beloved grandchild, and also watching their own child—now the parent—suffer the pain of losing a child.

It was shattering to stand by Trevor's bed and watch his systems close down and not be able to give him hope. It was a test to our faith to pray with agonizing earnestness—and to receive no apparent answer from heaven. It was difficult to speak of a God who really loved Trevor and his family. It was heart-rending to hear Trevor's own prayers for healing and to listen to him say, "Mommy, I don't want to die!"

But Trevor, our beloved grandson, died quietly after drifting off in a coma.

The journey that our daughter Sandy has taken since that day has been fraught with emotional experiences. Through reading, prayer, counseling, and heaven-sent judgment, she has come through the experience stronger, wiser, and able to find her place nearer to the heart of God.

Her mother and I have also been helped through the

dark tunnel into the light of God's abundant grace. Brighter now by a thousand times is the promise of our Lord's return. Greater than ever is our determination to be on God's side when Christ comes to reunite families and usher in that never-ending day.

Grandpa C. Lloyd Wyman

Hold Me
I Need to Be Carried

Section One

In the hour of trial,
Jesus, plead for me,
Lest by base denial
I depart from Thee;
When Thou see'st me waver,
With a look recall,
Nor, for fear or favor,
Suffer me to fall.

With forbidden pleasures,
Would this vain world charm;
Or its sordid treasures
Spread to work me harm;
Bring to my remembrance
Sad Gethsemane,
Or, in darker semblance,
Cross-crowned Calvary.

Should Thy mercy send me
Sorrow, toil, and woe,
Or should pain attend me
On my path below,
Grant that I may never
Fail Thy hand to see;
Grant that I may ever
Cast my care on Thee.

Chapter One

Everybody's Child

**"God loves each one of us as if there
were only one of us."**
—St. Augustine

"Can a woman forget her. . .child?"
—Isaiah 49:15, KJV

For as long as I can remember, I wanted to have children. I loved baby anythings—baby cats, baby dogs, baby animals in the zoo. I even brought home baby bugs. I was always enchanted by the innocence and dependency of young creatures.

I delighted in being around little children and even adored my own baby brother, Scott, who was 6 years younger. At least, I adored him until I turned 12 or 13, and then he was most definitely a nuisance to my all-important adolescent agendas!

When I discovered I was pregnant with my firstborn, I was ecstatic! Even the seven months of feeling green all day didn't dampen my eagerness to be a mother. To feel that little life inside was at the top of my list of life's greatest experiences.

I was fortunate to have only four hours of labor, with no medications, and was acutely aware of every ache and quiver as Todd came into the world. When I held him for the first time, it was a sacred moment. I remember a few days later thinking sadly that it wouldn't be long before he was in college. Now that he's 14, there are days when I wonder why it's taking so long!

What a precious privilege it is to be a parent! We begin dreaming and planning a future for our child from the first moment we lay eyes on him or her, as if somehow that little life belonged to us. We invest our time, our energy, our money and our hearts—and never for a moment allow ourselves to think about any future interruptions to our hopes and dreams.

I was still in this long-awaited and thoroughly enjoyed experience of parenting when Trevor arrived—three and a half years after his brother. I was sure I was carrying a girl, but when, after four hours of labor, the doctor announced, "It's a boy!" it was just the way it was supposed to be.

He was a beautiful baby, with all body parts perfectly intact—and he had red hair! No one for three generations on either side of the family had red hair. I remember he cried for 10 minutes, and then settled into being a happy, easy-to-please, contented baby—characteristics that would describe him for the next seven years of his life.

Trevor was everybody's child. His physical features were so attractive that people would stop and stare at him. That sandy red hair, big blue-green eyes and constant smile were disarming. And he just sort of bounced when he walked, full of anticipation for what the day would bring. He was a cuddler, and came in every morning to crawl into bed with us for "cuddle-time."

While he loved to be with people, he was also content to play alone and would entertain himself by the hour. He would stack the blocks up—and knock them down, only to do it again and again. He was patient and tolerant and flexible with how his day went. He was so easy to take care of that I sometimes thought that in all fairness I should pass him around to other parents, so they, too, would know the joys of parenting an "easy" baby.

Don't get me wrong—I absolutely adored Todd and could write volumes on his virtues as well, but most of the parenting books are written about Todd and other wonderful children like him. Those volumes concentrate on the challenges of parenting, and with Trevor, the challenge was to find something to be challenged about!

Oh, he was a normal child and wrote on the walls with crayons and whined when he had to go to bed. But there was also something different about him, and I used to watch him and wonder what his destiny would be.

It was evident early on that Trevor possessed an unusually endearing spirit. As people talk about him, they speak of how much he affected their lives, even as a little fellow. He had a sense of "others," and is still the only child I know who made out his list of what he wanted to *give* for Christmas before he made out the list for what he wanted to *get*. No one taught him to do that.

Trevor adored his older brother, and they were good buddies, although they had their "moments." Todd was the "can't sit still, gotta go" personality, full of energy. To this day he is one of the most physically coordinated boys I've ever seen. He's a natural at any sport he tries.

Trevor was reasonable in sports, but his special talents were creative. Trevor would come up with the mischievous idea, and Todd would carry it out, which did present challenges for uncovering who was *really* responsible. Those of you who are parents know exactly what I'm talking about.

One of Trevor's favorite things to do was to "dogpile" wrestle on the floor with his dad and brother. He always got a kick out of "winning" his dad.

My clearest memories of Trevor are of his skipping everywhere he went—whistling or humming—and always smiling. His "glass" was always "half full." He saw the good in things and in people. He was quick to offer encouragement, to say "thank you," and if he heard someone being criticized, he'd say something positive about that person.

One day when we were walking the dog I said, "Trevie, isn't it a beautiful day?" He replied, "Mommy, it would be a beautiful day even if it was raining!"

His insights and comments were well beyond his years. When we would be outside, or traveling in the car, he would notice things that none of the rest of us saw or heard. One day he and I were sitting on the front porch when he noticed a bird singing in a nearby tree. He proceeded to describe to me what the bird must be feeling because of the way it was singing. To Trevor, life was definitely worth living, and too short to miss any of it.

When he was 5 years old his little sister, Taryn, was born. Actually, she was rescued! She came into the world three and a half months early, weighing only 1 pound, 11 ounces.

It was a very stressful time for the family. I was flown by helicopter to a hospital two hours away, where I stayed for a week and then underwent an emergency Cesarean section to deliver her.

For the next three months we all went back and forth by car every weekend to be with Taryn in the neonatal-intensive-care unit. She was so tiny and fragile, yet feisty.

Each of us related to this tiny newcomer differently. It took each of us our own time to be willing to fall in love with her and risk the pain of possibly losing her.

Todd was older and more aware of the critical environment Taryn was in. He focused on the monitors, the beeps, and the alarms. He asked us if she was going to die.

Trevor simply pulled up a stool, opened the portholes of the incubator and softly rubbed her tiny back while he told her all about what it was like at home. He said he couldn't wait until she could leave the hospital and come back to

Santa Maria. He always told her how much he loved her.

One day as we were standing by her incubator, he looked up at me and said, "Mommy, when she comes home, I'll never be mean to her." And he never was.

Taryn came home when she was 88 days old. She weighed only five pounds, but had absolutely no health problems. Oh! how Trevor adored her. He played with her, read to her, and held her every chance he got. When he was holding her, he always had a beaming smile.

School was one of life's highlights for Trevor. On that first day of first grade you'd have thought he'd been chosen for a mission to the moon! He quickly made friends and came home every day with animated stories of the wonders of learning. I've been told that kids argued on the school bus over who got to sit with Trevor.

He had an excellent teacher for first grade, a deeply spiritual woman, and Trevor seemed quick to understand and accept spiritual values. Trevor was eager to trust and painfully honest.

Once I watched him sneaking some gum out of my dresser drawer. Later that day I said to him, "You know, Trevor, I was going to share some of my gum with you, but when I went to get it, it was all gone. I'm sorry." He said nervously, "That's okay Mom, thanks for wanting to share."

About 15 minutes later he was back, big tears filling his eyes. Out tumbled the whole truth, and then he asked if we could pray about it and ask Jesus to forgive him and help him not do it again. From that day on he always asked permission for things he wanted.

Trevor had a way of bringing out the best in others and inspiring them to fulfill their highest calling. Trevor truly was everybody's child and everybody's friend. When you stop to think about it, each of us is everybody's child. We're all connected to each other in ways we don't even begin to understand. What happens to you affects me, and what happens to me affects you.

So Trevor was your child, too. I want to share his story so that your life can be touched and changed, as was mine. Many times I felt like I learned more from this little man than I taught him. But at the beginning, how could I have known what Trevor's highest calling would be?

Chapter Two

So Much Dizziness

"The Lord will guide you always; he will satisfy your needs in a sun-scorched land and will strengthen your frame. You will be like a well-watered garden, like a spring whose waters never fail."
—*Isaiah 58:11, NIV*

In January I got a call from the school principal, who reported that Trevor had thrown up on the school bus on the way back from a field trip. During that month he had a few more episodes of car sickness.

He also described feeling "funny" after being in the bathtub for a few minutes, as if he were overheating easily. While he was eating or doing schoolwork, I noticed a subtle, slight tremor of his left hand when he'd reach for things. He had an ear infection and cold with the usual symptoms; the other symptoms would come and go without any real patterns.

One day when we were in the car Trevor said, "Mommy, I see two of you. And I see two cars and two trees." I asked him if things had looked like that the day before, and he said no. A few days later I asked him if he was seeing two of things, and he said no.

I recall I felt uneasy at the time. Every nurse will admit that when her child is feeling sick, for a few moments she thinks the worst. Then she reminds herself that 95 percent of the time kids' symptoms don't signify serious illness.

Then one Friday afternoon I saw Trevor watching TV with one eye covered. I said, "Trevie, what are you doing?" He said, "Well, if I cover one eye, then I don't see two TVs."

I was concerned enough to make an appointment for the following week with an optometrist.

That weekend we joined several other young families for a potluck lunch after church. The children were all outside playing, running up a hill. I'll never forget the look on Trevor's face as he came into the room and tried to describe the dizziness he felt after running up the hill. His face was pale, and his eyes told me he was afraid.

We left the potluck and took him to see the pediatrician on call. His exam showed nothing out of the ordinary. We were sent home to observe.

Wednesday we had the appointment with the optometrist. She examined Trevor and "couldn't put her finger on it," but she referred us to a pediatric ophthalmologist. We were able to get an appointment with the specialist that Friday.

While Trevor and I sat in her office waiting room, Trevor laid his head on my lap, and I realized that in the last few days he'd seemed more tired than usual. Maybe he was just catching a virus of some kind. I stroked his thick red hair and allowed myself only 10 seconds of thinking that something serious could be happening.

The ophthalmologist was very thorough and put us at ease with her friendly, competent exam. She said that Trevor did not show any signs of pressure behind his eyes, which was good, but she did notice the nystagmus, which I had not noticed. (Nystagmus is a condition where the eyes jump back and forth when looking to the extreme right or left.)

The tremor of his left hand was more pronounced, and she recommended that we have an urgent magnetic resonance imaging (MRI) scan to rule out anything serious. She gave the impression that everything would be fine.

She made a few phone calls, and we were scheduled for

an MRI the next day, March 18. That was my birthday, and my parents were visiting with us at our home in Santa Maria, California. It was good to have their presence and support at this stressful time.

In the waiting room of the radiology department, Trevor experienced a dizzy spell and threw up on the carpet that had just been installed. I felt so badly for him, and wished it could be me having to go through this. (Of course, since I worked at this hospital, I'd have never heard the end of throwing up on the new carpet!)

Trevor was sedated so that he could be perfectly still for 45 minutes in the MRI chamber. He did well, and we brought him home. He slept, while the rest of us sat around staring at the phone.

If you've ever waited for the result of a serious test, you know what I mean when I say we stared at the phone. After what seemed like an eternity, the telephone rang, and the radiologist on the other end of the line said those beloved words, *"The MRI result is negative!"*

Oh, the rejoicing and hollering that went on for the next few minutes! We thanked God for the results and embraced our feelings of relief while Trevor slept.

I remember thinking about how quick we are to praise God when things go the way we want them to. How wonderful and merciful He is—as long as everything is going well. "Could it be that He is still being wonderful and merciful, even when tragic things happen?" I was surely glad that I didn't have to struggle with that question right now because Trevor was going to be okay!

But over the next weeks I began to dread waking up in the morning. Each day brought a new progression in the pattern of symptoms that Trevor was developing. Almost every day there would be an episode of dizziness, followed by vomiting. I noticed that he seemed to lean to the left just slightly when walking.

One day my husband said to me, "Don't you think that Trev's speech is a little slower? He seems like he's not talking as fast as usual." I had to admit I hadn't noticed. I think there were things I just didn't want to see.

One day as Trevor was eating breakfast he said, "Mommy, when I swallow, it feels like little bubbles in my throat."

I was concerned enough to pursue further evaluation. The pediatrician suggested we go see an ENT—ear, nose, and throat specialist. The specialist recommended another MRI scan, this time with contrast dye, so the doctors could better see the sinuses.

And so we endured another scan. They discovered an area of consolidation in his sinuses; however the doctor couldn't really explain Trevor's symptoms based on the location of this finding.

We were referred to a neurologist, and a few days later we saw him. By this time Trevor wanted to lie down all the time. He said he "felt funny" when he was up. His speech was also becoming slightly nasal.

The neurologist reviewed the two MRI scans and did a thorough examination. He recognized Trevor was fatigued, but didn't feel the signs were ominous. Nevertheless, he recommended that we see a pediatric neurologist.

Trevor's appetite was diminishing, and he'd lost 10 pounds off his solid little muscular body. By this time we'd taken him out of school, which he missed very much.

He spent much of his day watching TV or reading, although he was seeing double continuously. Whatever it was that was causing his problems was affecting only his motor skills. His thinking processes were not diminished. He was as sharp and clever as ever, always coming up with his trademark one-liners that would set everyone at ease.

We made arrangements to see the pediatric neurologist, Mark Corazza, MD, who was highly recommended. The doctor spent a lot of time examining Trevor, putting him through a battery of motor-skill tests. Obviously he was concerned, and whatever this was, it wasn't right out of the medical textbooks. Dr. Corazza recommended more tests. We found ourselves facing another MRI, a lumbar puncture, an EMG (electromyography) and other difficult tests.

To prevent severe dizziness and vomiting, Trevor had to lie down all the time. His daddy would carry him flat—like an airplane—out to the van, keeping him as level as possible. How I hated to see Trevor like that! More than once he vomited in the van on the 90-minute trip to Sansum Clinic in Santa Barbara. His speech was getting more difficult to understand, and he was taking more care in swallowing.

It was nearing the end of April, and it was time for our second appointment with the pediatric neurologist. At this visit he was going to give us the results of all of the tests.

For this second appointment, Trevor had to be taken upstairs on a gurney. It was just Trevor and me at this appointment, and the doctor took me in to look at the MRI scan.

Even I could see a patchy area of white in his left cerebellum. The neurologist felt it was encephalitis, an inflammatory condition of the brain, that with treatment should be resolved, most likely 100 percent in a child. Trevor had been through a series of hepatitis vaccines in January, and the working consensus was that he was having a severe autoimmune reaction to the vaccines.

Dr. Corazza recommended that we admit Trevor to the hospital so he could be started on high doses of steroids to reduce the cerebral inflammation. We admitted our boy to the hospital, fully confident that with treatment he'd recover and we'd have an end to this ordeal.

In the hospital in Santa Barbara Trevor underwent more tests and was hooked up to IVs. Every day different specialists came in to evaluate and try to rehabilitate him.

Speech therapists worked with him to exercise the speech muscles. (His speech was similar to someone with a cleft palate.) Evidently the palate on the roof of his mouth wasn't moving. Trevor worked faithfully on his mouth exercises.

Physical therapists tried to get Trevor into different positions. Sitting up was difficult for Trevor. He'd been lying on his right side for more than a month now, and he was developing contractors of his neck—a shortening of the muscles from lack of use.

Yet through all of this he never complained. The nurses and therapists quickly fell in love with his constant smile, sweet spirit, and willingness to keep trying.

Trevor enjoyed the visitors who streamed in to see him. Had you come to visit him, he'd have offered you candy; had you brought him a gift, he'd have been quick to tell me to write you a thank-you note.

We did a lot of things together. Trevor loved crafts and coloring. It was painful to watch him put Legos together with his left hand shaking and his eyes seeing double.

These activities were hard for him to do—lying on his right side all the time—but he exhibited such an acceptance of what he was going through. One day he said to me, "Mommy, I always thought this would happen to me when I got old, but not when I would be a kid."

It was nearing Mother's Day, and he was sad he couldn't get me something, so we made a pretend flower arrangement with the hospital pitcher, pipe cleaners and paper medicine cups that we painted red. I'll never forget the smile on his face when we were finished, and he told me I was the best mom in the world.

After two weeks in the hospital plans were being arranged to send him home. Trevor was so excited! The steroids had improved the tremor of his left hand, and the nystagmus was less in his eyes.

The physical therapists even got him to take a few steps with help. Medication had reduced the vomiting, and the steroids had returned his appetite, which was so good to see. He worked slowly and hard to position the food just right on the right side of his mouth so he could work it back to swallow it safely.

However, he still couldn't sit longer than two minutes on the side of the bed before the dizziness came over him. He still couldn't lie flat with his head up toward the ceiling.

We'd arranged for a hospital bed at home. Physical and speech therapy services would be provided every day for continued rehabilitation. Home health aides would be there eight hours a day so that I could go back to work some.

Trevor came home on May 13, the day before his seventh birthday. The next day his whole first-grade class came on a field trip to see him. They'd been praying for him every day, and I just knew that their sweet prayers had been answered.

Trevor was all smiles, so happy was he to see his friends. He opened their gifts; his favorite was Ninja Turtles. We had cake and ice cream and all talked about second grade next year, when Trevor would be back in school again.

We began a planned program of rehabilitation at home. Trevor and I created a scorecard where he recorded points and worked for a prize. His activities included mouth exercises, range-of-motion exercises, and trying to sit on the edge of the bed every day. This daily itinerary of activities and exercises kept us all busy.

Trevor had to use a bedpan and urinal, and we created a buzzer system so that I could attend to his needs at night. He always apologized for disturbing me.

I washed his hair and bathed him in bed every day. He loved to have his feet and back rubbed. Taryn, who was 2, would climb up on the bed with him, and he would read to her and play with her. To this day she remembers him feeding her French fries and ketchup up on that hospital bed.

One day Trevor asked one of his aides, "Joyce, do you know Jesus?" She answered, "Well, yes, I do!"

Trevor said, "I thought so, but I wanted to make sure,

'cuz it's important!"

After about two weeks at home Trevor began to ask me several times a day if we could pray together. He'd always been sensitive to spiritual things, but during this illness he hadn't wanted to pray, although it was okay for me to say our good-night prayers. Now he wanted to pray together often. I realized later he knew something was not right.

Trevor never got beyond being able to sit on the edge of the bed for more than three minutes. When he tried to walk, he leaned heavily to the left, and he couldn't take more than 10 steps with help.

I'd ask him how he felt and he'd say, "I can't describe it; I just don't feel *right*."

The high doses of steroids had made him puffy, and his sweet little face looked different. My heart ached as I watched how hard he worked to get better. I'd have given anything for it to be me instead suffering so.

One Friday morning I prepared his pills as usual in the seedless jam that made it easier for him to swallow. He took them into his mouth, but he was unable to swallow them. He tried again, but they wouldn't go down.

He looked at me and said, "Mommy, I'm not getting any better; I think we'd better call the doctor."

I was in a state of denial about the lack of progress. After all, we'd had four MRI scans and a host of other tests. Medical consensus about his condition was that he would get better. But I was suddenly forced to admit that Trevor was right; he was *not* getting well.

I called Dr. Corazza. We'd talked to him every few days, but as I described Trevor's inability to swallow that morning, he said, "If this is encephalitis, he should have made his turn by now. I think you'd better bring him back to the hospital so we can get a handle on this."

Trevor had been home only three weeks.

Chapter Three

Stop This Train—
I Want To Get Off!

**"For the thing which I greatly feared is come upon
me,
and that which I was afraid of is come unto me.
I was not in safety, neither had I rest, neither was
I quiet; yet trouble came."**
—Job 3:25-26, KJV

We admitted Trevor to the hospital again, and a fifth MRI
scan was ordered that same day. This time I was truly scared.

I've been a nurse for 22 years, and much of that time I've
worked in intensive-care units and emergency rooms. I've
been through traumatic and tragic hours with patients and
families, and they've taught me much about the most effective and healing way to embark on such a journey.

Yet suddenly I found myself in personally uncharted
territory. My mind was jumping ahead again, wondering if
the worst scenario was about to be played out in our lives.

Trevor underwent the MRI scan. By now he was telling
the technicians how to do it! Intravenous infusions were
started, and yet more tests were done. And we *waited.* . .

I remember as we rolled Trevor out of the MRI room, five

physician specialists were looking at his films. I caught a quick glance at their faces, and they were obviously concerned. They were all talking and pointing to the films and shaking their heads. I started to feel sick.

We took Trevor back to his room. Transferring him from gurney to bed had to be done carefully, with four or five people helping so we could keep him flat and on his right side in order to avoid violent dizziness. When he was comfortable, my husband and I went into the waiting room.

I know now why they call them *waiting rooms*. What seemed like an eternity was actually only about 45 minutes. Dr. Corazza came into the room. He had tears in his eyes as he began to speak, and I felt my heart literally skip beats. I was stiff as a board, and what he said next seemed like it was in slow motion and echoing from a tunnel.

"I w-i-s-h I d-i-d-n-'t h-a-v-e t-o t-e-l-l y-o-u t-h-i-s, b-u-t i-t a-p-p-e-a-r-s T-r-e-v-o-r h-a-s a p-o-n-t-i-n-e b-r-a-i-n-s-t-e-m g-l-i-o-b-l-a-s-t-o-m-a."

The doctor's voice continued. "I-t's t-h-e f-a-s-t-e-s-t g-r-o-w-i-n-g c-a-n-c-e-r t-h-e-r-e i-s, i-n t-h-e w-o-r-s-t p-l-a-c-e y-o-u c-a-n h-a-v-e i-t."

Again I heard his voice coming from the tunnel. "A-n-d I-'m a-f-r-a-i-d i-t-'s n-o-t o-p-e-r-a-b-l-e!"

Then we asked him the agonizing question I've heard many of my patients ask.

And he answered, "M-a-y-b-e a f-e-w w-e-e-k-s."

Pow! I felt like I'd been hit by a truck. The room was heavy, as if someone had sucked out all the air. I remember not knowing if I was going to take my next breath.

* * * * *

In those initial moments my entire life flashed in front of me. I saw myself as the little girl who grew up singing songs about God's unfailing goodness and mercy, who memorized scriptures about how God sees and answers every prayer. I recalled my earliest concept of God.

My father, Pastor Lloyd Wyman, started his life of ministry in singing evangelism. I was probably about 4 or 5 years old, and I remember seeing slide pictures of Jesus the Good Shepherd, holding a lamb. My parents sang a song together entitled "That One Lost Sheep."

> *Safe were the ninety and nine in the fold,*
> *Safe, though the night was stormy and cold;*
> *But said the shepherd, when counting them o'er,*
> *"One sheep is missing. There should be one more!"*
> *The shepherd went out to search for his sheep,*
> *And all thro' the night on the rocky steep*
> *He sought till he found him,*
> *with love-bands he bound him,*
> *And I was that one lost sheep.*

I had fallen in love with this compassionate God, who values each one as worth any cost. It was easy for me to embrace this consoling concept because I had a consistently loving and nurturing earthly father whom I adored and who daily practiced what he preached.

But my adult life had not always found me fully surrendered to God as Lord of my life. So much of the time I got by on my solid upbringing, good personality, and seeming capability. All of those things, of course, are abundant gifts from God—but how easy it was to take the driver's seat and be my own final authority on things.

In that moment of truth, my mistakes and wrong-doings flashed before me and I found myself quickly and desperately asking for forgiveness, claiming scripture like it was some sort of magic, and recalling Bible stories where Christ performed healing miracles. I was frantically search-ing for that perfect response that would *make* God do a miracle for us. . .

"Oh, please, stop this train so I can get off! I don't want to do this—anything but this!" I cried inside.

I was afraid I couldn't handle it, yet at the same time I was angry because I knew somehow, that I *would* make it through. I didn't want to make it through—I wanted the circumstances to change!

The temptation was great to make this tragedy all about *me*: This was happening because I hadn't been good enough; I needed more faith; I needed to be taught a lesson. . .

While I believed that God was in the business of developing character, I did know that these self-centered assumptions were fear-based. I wanted a grand *reason*, some sort of explanation that would make sense out of this horrifying pain.

My grandparents were missionaries in Burma, where my father was born and raised. I grew up listening to stories of missionaries who were killed for their convictions. I knew that God's ways are not our ways and that His purposes are often advanced through persecution and trial. That made sense to me—having a cause you believe in and dying for it is an honorable thing.

But what sense did *this* make? And since I was asking *that* question—what about the plane crashes, the drive-by shootings, the innocent children kidnapped and tortured? I was demanding answers, and felt only silence.

I knew that whatever it was I believed—and had been speaking about all my life—now had to be taken back to square one. Now was when it would really matter. Either what I'd believed about God was the greatest reality of the universe or it was the biggest scam ever played on human beings. Which was it? If I'd felt God's presence with me in good times, would I be willing to trust that He was just as fully with me in such a nightmare?

* * * * *

We went in and told Trevor right away. I said "Trevie, the doctor looked again at the pictures of the inside of your head. He says there's a spot that is growing in there that's not normal. It's actually a very small spot. It's called a *tumor*. He said that people who have this kind of tumor usually do not live very long."

("Oh God, I can't believe this is real! Maybe I'll wake up and it will have been a horrible nightmare.")

I felt his little hand grab mine. Trevor started to cry. We all cried and held each other for many minutes. Then, while patting me on the back, he said, "Well, at least I've lived 7 years—some people don't even have that!"

And so began what I now believe was the Holy Spirit's effective work on us all through Trevor, because he was trusting and ready.

About an hour later, after having called our family members, I telephoned a friend, Karen Nicola. Karen and her husband, Steve, had lost a beautiful little 5-year-old son to leukemia a few years before.

I said, "Karen, how do you do this? I didn't take any classes for this, and I have no strategies to pull out of my hat." Her response became the best counsel I received.

She said, "Sandy, this may sound cold to you now, but what you need to do is to *lean in to it*—don't resist, don't run. If this is to be your journey, it will take you to places in your soul you could never go otherwise. *Be in every moment*, embrace every moment as a gift. God will see you through this. Hope and pray for physical healing, but know that God's best plan will be accomplished."

I was numb. Although I couldn't fully accept everything she was saying, it was time for me to start "leaning into it."

That afternoon I went into the nurses' lounge and looked out the window at the lavish view of Santa Barbara. Life was teeming out there. I wondered how many others were also screaming out in defiance at the "cards" life had dealt them.

I felt detached from myself. I knew that I'd be living one hour at a time for who knows how long, and I wondered who I would be a few months from now. The choices ahead were not visible.

Later that evening Dr. Corazza stopped by to check on us. He and I had a touching discussion. He has four young children of his own, one of them a boy about Trevor's age. He was identifying closely with our experience.

We shared a common faith in God, and our belief that life here is a short journey compared to all of eternity that is ours because of Jesus Christ. As I talked and cried, I knew I believed these things, but I also knew that my confidence and trust in them was about to be put through the fire—and I trembled.

Chapter Four

Three Hundred Sixty Hours

**"God is our refuge and strength,
an ever present help in trouble.
Therefore we will not fear, though the earth give way
and the mountains fall into the heart of the sea."**
—Psalm 46: 1-2, NIV

**"I would rather walk with God in the dark
than go alone in the light."**
—Mary Gardiner Brainard

That night after hearing Trevor's diagnosis I lay on the cot beside his bed not knowing what to think or feel. My mind was a blur, my body was exhausted, my soul was numb. My few moments of dozing were interrupted by Trevor's requests to use the urinal or have a drink of water.

In the darkness of night I thought that if I could just get really real with God and be fully surrendered to *His* will, that *my* desires would be granted—sort of like rubbing the genie bottle. I did not realize how I was trying to manipulate God.

Early the next morning there was a commotion out by the nurses' station. Four or five physician specialists had gathered to discuss Trevor's case. They seemed to have consensus about the type of tumor we were dealing with, yet most of them had no first-hand experience with it.

I was later to learn that this type of tumor occurs only in children aged 6 to 10, and only in about 100 children a year throughout the world. It is always fatal, usually within six months. The physicians were beginning to make phone calls, connecting with specialists familiar with the cancer to try to determine what the current treatment options were.

Someone in our church congregation had contacted the office of Dr. Fred Epstein, world-renowned pediatric neurosurgeon at New York University. This physician has been written about in many journals and has authored his own book. He is known for successfully going after the most difficult tumors.

At 6:30 that morning a nurse came into my room and said, "Dr. Epstein is on the phone for you." I had no idea how this doctor had known to call me. I knew who he was because one of the nurses had brought his book to me the evening before. I was stunned he was calling me.

I went down the hall to the phone and began speaking with a most endearing gentleman. He listened to my explanation of the clinical findings as I understood them, then asked if I could immediately send him copies of Trevor's MRI scans. My heart began to race. This could be it! The answer to prayer!

We also contacted Dr. Ben Carson, world-renowned pediatric neurosurgeon at Johns Hopkins University, and a fellow church member. He, too, was interested in viewing the MRI scans.

We scurried to get copies of the scans made. We sent them to Dr. Epstein and Dr. Carson, as well as to the medical schools at Loma Linda University and UCLA.

Within 24 hours I had personally spoken with these specialists, and they all confirmed the diagnosis that we'd been given. Both Dr. Epstein and Dr. Carson were sorrowful, but explained that this was one tumor that they could not go after surgically.

A glioma blends in with healthy tissue, like liquid creamer added to a hot drink. If the glioma is in certain other parts of the brain, sometimes that area can be successfully resected and the patient has a good chance of recovery. Other types of consolidated tumors can be removed from the brain stem.

But a glioma in the brain stem—well, our technology just isn't there yet. The brain stem houses our center for breathing and is the relay for all other information traveling to and from the brain. We can't survive with *any* of it removed.

We were advised that radiation treatments were our only hope. There was a small chance—5 to 10 percent—that it would be successful enough to add a few months to Trevor's life. The more realistic hope was that it would alleviate the severe dizziness he was experiencing so that he could be more comfortable for whatever time he had left.

Talking about the options a mere 48 hours after hearing the diagnosis made me nauseated, but I found myself in a survival mode, going through the motions and just doing the next indicated thing.

Phone calls began coming from well-meaning people who suggested alternative methods of treatment. Some were bizarre. One caller said, "You should go down to Mexico to this clinic where they inject people with lizard urine. . ."

As a Christian I understood this life is not all there is, so I didn't feel the need to run around the world searching for anything that might work. However, I did wonder just what might be out there. There was some promising research being done in Florida by a specialist who had worked with 12 children with similar tumors. Here's how the treatment went:

The child had his bone marrow removed, then was given massive doses of chemotherapy for seven days. The bone marrow was then replaced. After that the child was placed in a laminar-flow unit for six weeks. During that time no one could visit him, as he was at extremely high risk for infections. The patient then underwent radiation treatments.

Two of the children treated with this regimen were rendered tumor-free one year later. Most of the others either died of infections—or the progression of their tumor.

We opted not to undergo such extreme measures. We didn't want to withhold treatment that might work, yet we didn't wish to increase Trevor's suffering with a "long shot." We decided to proceed immediately with radiation.

I didn't know it then, but this was the beginning of our final 15 days together—just 360 hours!

Trevor had to undergo radiation treatments twice daily. We were told that his thick red hair would probably fall out around his ears and the sides of his head in a week or so.

Radiation was hard on him, especially the moving from the bed to the treatment table and back again. The first day was especially difficult because nuclear medicine technicians had to make a foam impression of his head, neck, and shoulders so that he would fit perfectly into it during each subsequent treatment. (Exact positioning is important because the radiation must be aimed precisely at the part of the brain stem where the tumor is.)

But despite the discomfort, Trevor was always smiling. The people in nuclear medicine fell in love with him. Even through waves of dizziness he always had a quick little remark to lighten the moment.

Sometimes on the way back to his room from a treatment we'd go up to the sixth floor, which had a lovely balcony overlooking Santa Barbara. The view of the town—and the ocean beyond—was beautiful and peaceful, and Trevor enjoyed getting outside for a short time.

It was hard to watch his little body changing as a result of taking steroids and the effects of bed rest. His face and tummy were puffy; his arms and legs were getting smaller from muscle loss. Watching him drool, and work so hard to eat and swallow safely, and listening to his slurred speech. . .it was almost too much for me.

Would I ever hear his normal speech again. . .or hear him sing in his own sweet voice. . .or see him walk or run? Would I ever be able to hold him while he was standing up, or feel him wrap both arms around me? What would Todd and Taryn do without him? Haunting fears of the unknown raced through me.

But there were ordinary times, too. Trevor and I spent our days together reading and doing crafts. I had a drawing book that he loved. I'd trace the shape of his hand or fist, then draw an animal out of that tracing for him to color. He got others involved in his projects, too. Trevor always asked his visitors to make something out of pipe cleaners to leave on the windowsill with the other works of art.

Someone sent us a Bible storybook about heaven, and Trevor enjoyed having me read it to him. With his double vision he couldn't read much any more.

The Make-A-Wish Foundation came to see him a few days after he was hospitalized. They told him their purpose was to grant him any wish he desired—and I knew what his response would be. He just couldn't think of anything he wanted to do, because he was a child who was always content. He couldn't imagine anything that would be better than what he was doing at the time, particularly if he were doing it with his family.

His first request was to go home, be with his family, and be well. How they wished they could grant that one! Then Trevor came up with two ideas. One was to have someone who knew origami, the Japanese art of paper folding, come and make things for him. They said they would do that.

Then, showing his very human side, he asked if he could have the whole Toys-R-Us store reserved for him after hours. They said that could be done—and that he could have whatever he wanted from the store. When they said that, Trevor smiled and retorted, "I'd still rather go home."

(Ironically, though the Make-A-Wish Foundation did set

up dates for the origami demonstration and the Toys-R-Us shopping excursion, they were scheduled too far in advance. Trevor was dead before they could be fulfilled.)

The entire wall of his hospital room was filled with cards and letters from loving friends and family. Many visitors came to share memories with Trevor. His face would light up as he'd remember the good times, sometimes through pictures they'd brought. It was difficult to watch the pain in their faces as they glanced back one more time before leaving the room, knowing it might be the last time they'd see him.

We both loved to sing, and we sang together often. He'd say, "Mom, I've got this song in my head and I can't get it to stop, so we'd better sing it." He wasn't able to carry a tune any longer, and the words didn't come out sounding quite the same, but he had the same bright spirit. To keep time he'd tap his hands or feet on the bed.

During Trevor's first hospitalization he'd wanted to sing songs like "Take Me Out to the Ball Game," "There's a Hole in the Bottom of the Sea," and "Do Your Ears Hang Low?" Now he chose songs like, "It's Me, O Lord," "Do Lord," and his favorite, "He's Able." We sang it together many times.

All our hopes and dreams were in our hearts as we sang that song together. I believe that God performs physical healings today, but that most of the time it is not His response to do so. Would I still want to trust and serve Him if I were one who was just "carried through," and not the recipient of a miracle?

I was helped by one special conversation with my father. He said, "Let's stop sorrowing over this boy as if he were gone. He's alive *now*. If he should be laid to rest, there'll be plenty of time to sorrow then. Don't borrow sorrow from tomorrow. Let's keep hope alive—and storm the gates of heaven with our petitions." I liked that.

Every day Trevor and I took time to talk about things we were thankful for. It was amazing how that helped to boost my spirit. Trevor and I talked about heaven and what we were looking forward to the most, and then we'd cry.

He said, "Mommy, if I die, for me it won't be so hard, 'cuz the next thing I know, I'll see Jesus and you, and all my family. But for you, Mommy, it will be so hard. I don't want you to have to miss me."

Through my tears I'd watch while he slept, memorizing each little freckle, each long eyelash, and wondering how I was going to go on without him. When he'd wake up and see my tears, he'd reach out for me, hug me, and tell me it would be okay. I told him how my heart was breaking, but that I knew God loved him more than I did, because he really belonged to God and not to me. And I promised Trevor that others would know of his struggle and faith.

He told the nurses how he loved his family, and he thanked them for all their help. It was clear the nurses had a special place in their hearts for this little boy with dancing eyes who passed on grace and courage to everyone.

Sometimes I didn't know what do with myself. Much of the time was spent with Trevor, but while he was napping I noticed how meaningless everything else seemed. I wanted every moment to count, to somehow be extraordinary, but there were so many ordinary tasks to be done.

I tried to stay in each moment, but hanging over me like a descending dark blanket was the constant awareness of an unknown date and time when this beautiful little child of mine would take his last breath. Even though I'd been losing weight from the stress, I felt as if I weighed 100 pounds more from the heaviness of the sorrow.

My parents came after they'd finished walking the half marathon in Lompoc, a town north of Santa Barbara. My mom received a medal, and she gave it to Trevor, telling him he was in a marathon of his own. She said, "The difference is that Jesus can run this one for you, and carry you— and the finish line is heaven! Even if you take a little 'nap' (death) the finish line is still heaven."

During this time our church had two all-night prayer vigils for Trevor. They spent the night singing, claiming Scripture, and praying together. In fact, churches all over the country were praying for him. Somehow the word got out and even the staff at our church's world headquarters were having special prayer for Trevor. If answered prayer is about numbers, then we certainly had that on our side!

Actually, if it had been God's intention to physically heal Trevor, I believe He would have done it based on Trevor's prayers alone. They were the sweetest prayers of trust and honesty, and he prayed them three or four times a day.

"Dear Heavenly Father, please come and place your hands on the sick place in my head so I can get well and go home. I know I can't make myself well. I don't want to die. I want to trust you, Jesus, for whatever happens, because you know best. Please help all the children in the world to get well. I'm scared, so please help me. In Jesus' name I pray, amen."

And Trevor and I talked. Conversations such as this one I tucked into my memory: In the hospital gift shop I bought Trevor a troll doll holding its baby. Trevor said that it was me and him. He promised, "I'm gonna keep it till it turns to dust. I wouldn't sell it for a hundred million bucks."

"Some things are more important than money," I agreed.

"Love in your heart is most important." Trevor said.

After he'd been in the hospital for about four days he remembered the butterfly larvae that he'd left at home. A few weeks before he'd ordered a butterfly garden with money he'd been saving. The package arrived between hospitalizations, while he was at home those three weeks.

Five little larvae arrived in a glass jar with filter paper over the opening. There was about an inch of brown slimy stuff on the bottom of the jar. The package insert said that the larvae would eat the slime for a few days, get fatter, then climb to the top of the jar and attach themselves to the filter paper. Then they would spin their cocoons and we were to peel the filter paper off the jar and place it with the cocoons attached in a viewing box that they had sent.

When the butterflies emerged, we were to watch them for a few days and then let them go. Right! I had my doubts as to the success of all this, but Trevor was convinced the experiment would work, and he was excited about it.

The larvae had just gone to the top of the jar and spun cocoons when Trevor was re-admitted. Now he was concerned he might die and not be able to see them come out.

So I went home to Santa Maria and peeled off the filter paper and taped it to the inside of the viewing box. Now for the trick of safely getting them to Santa Barbara in the back of the van. The cocoons—each one hanging by a thread—flapped in the viewing box with every jolt of the van. Despite my skepticism, they all made it safely. Trevor was so happy to see them again.

I put the viewing box on his bedstand where he could see it. Soon word got out all over the hospital that there was a little boy up on pediatrics who was growing butterflies. Trevor's room became a daily stop-off place for hospital staff. Respiratory therapists, pharmacists, doctors, nurses, X-ray technicians, laboratory personnel—all would come by each day and ask, "Are they out yet?"

On a Wednesday the butterflies—beautiful little painted ladies—came out of their cocoons, one at a time, about 30 minutes apart. I had never seen such a thing, and I was in awe. Trevor's whole face lit up. Soon his room was full of admirers, and we had an impromptu butterfly party.

We watched the butterflies for two days, and then on Friday we took them up to the sixth floor balcony to let them go. Trevor opened the box—and the butterflies flew away one at a time, about two minutes apart.

Although he was weak, Trevor smiled as he turned to me and said, "Mommy, the caterpillars are like our lives here on earth; the cocoons are like when we die; and the butterflies are like when Jesus comes and we go to heaven!" Profound insight from this boy speaking well beyond his 7 years!

We had an anointing service for Trevor. Just a handful of special people: my parents, Pastor and Mrs. Lloyd Wyman; our pastor, Ken Lockwood, and his wife; Pastor Leslie Hardinge; and Pastor Lewis Lyman. We read scripture and sang songs, including Trevor's favorite, "Jesus Loves Me."

Amidst our tears, we each prayed, including Trevor. Then we placed our hands on Trevor and gave him over to the God of the universe. In my pain I had—for the first time— a very real sense that God was in this ordeal, that He was near, that He could be trusted no matter what happened.

However, I realize now that I was still busy setting God's agenda for Him. My prayers were full of reminders to Him of what a perfect stage had been set for Him to be glorified:

- No doctor could take credit for this healing;

- Thousands were praying, including Trevor's first-grade class, who started every morning praying for their friend;

- Flyers were circulated all over town by our neighbors, requesting prayers and donations to a trust fund;

- Everyone was hungry for a demonstration of God's healing power.

I read something especially meaningful a few days later: "How often it is that we fill out our page of agenda for God, and we graciously give it to Him to sign; when what we must do is sign a blank page and give it to Him to fill out."

This struggle to give our entire lives to God is at the very core of our beings. Until I was able to give Him my signed blank page, I could never have peace.

Chapter Five

The Blessing of the Stone

"We may be sure if God sends us on stony paths, He will not send us out on any journey for which He does not equip us well."
—Author unknown

During the first week of Trevor's rehospitalization he developed a kidney stone. This rarely happens in children. It was caused by weeks of immobilization and dehydration. Finally Trevor faced severe pain.

Prior to developing the kidney stone, he'd suffered from severe dizziness and had been confined to one position, but he'd had little pain. Now the dancing light in his eyes began to dim, and his smile wasn't as broad. He never complained, just drew up his legs and pointed to his stomach. His appetite disappeared, and I could tell he was frightened.

As parents we endure different kinds of agony over our children. Watching your child frightened and in severe pain, when you're helpless to fix it, is torture of the worst kind.

Now the reality began to sink in. *The inevitable is going to happen; Trevor is going to die.* It seemed as if the more we prayed. . .the harder we prayed. . .the more people who prayed, the faster he was deteriorating.

I was so angry with God about the kidney stone! *"Hasn't Trevor suffered enough already?"* I cried out in my agony. *"What is going on here, God? Why the pain? How can a greater good be served by letting this loving, spiritual child go? What a story of healing he would have to tell! He wants to grow up to be a kind, good man for you, Lord—don't you need people like him here on the earth?"*

While traveling back home to visit my other children, I'd pray aloud in my car, wrestling with God. I don't even remember driving. Sometimes I'd have to pull over and stop because I'd be crying so hard I couldn't see the road.

For the first time in my life, I got *real* with God and poured out my raw feelings—my anger, confusion, fear, and helplessness. Something began to happen in me as a result of honest confrontation. I felt God's presence with me and His assurance that I could trust Him with the outcome—that He had Trevor's best interest at heart as well as mine. It didn't take away the pain, but it did begin to bring peace.

I found that if I allowed myself to think too far ahead, trying to imagine how this would all play out, I'd get panicky and fearful again. I realized this was because God was not "out there." I came to understand that He'll be *there* when I get *there*, but He's only here in this moment. His strength and grace are for *this* moment. I needed to learn to stay in the moment; I began to take one hour at a time.

The evening after we let the butterflies go, my husband and I went to dinner while Trevor slept. When we returned there were many nurses in Trevor's room, surrounding his bed. My heart sank. Trevor had had a small focal seizure—his legs and face had spasmed. When we came into the room he was sleeping, as people do after having a seizure.

Blood was drawn to determine if there was any chemical imbalance, but the doctor suspected this was simply the progression of the tumor. Earlier that day a urologist had been called to evaluate the best option for dealing with the kidney stone, which was an adult-sized stone. There were no laser fields established for children, so breaking up the stone with a laser—a relatively new and less painful option in treating kidney stones—was not feasible.

The only sure option was to do major abdominal surgery to remove the stone. This would have meant general anesthesia with an endotracheal tube. Physicians feared they might not be able to get Trevor off the respirator, and he would die hooked to the machine. No one wanted to pursue this option on a terminally ill child, so we'd all been waiting, giving Trevor narcotics—which depress the brain stem—to mask the pain.

Trevor slept through the night until Saturday morning. When he awoke, he wasn't the same. His mind was as sharp, but it was as if he'd suffered a stroke. Now, for the first time, I couldn't understand what he was trying to say. I'd been the one interpreting for him, because others couldn't make out the words. Now even I was unable to understand, although he was trying very hard to communicate and sounds were coming out of his mouth.

I brought him a clipboard, but when he tried to write, all his letters went on top of each other.

He started to cry, and our tears mingled. We began to realize that we were in the closing hours together.

Trevor pointed to the 8 x 10 family portrait that was in his windowsill. I brought it to him, and he touched each person's face and cried with wrenching sobs.

"Trevie, do you want to see Todd and Taryn today?" I asked. He nodded yes. He adored his older brother and cherished his little sister. They were scheduled to come down the next day, Father's Day. We notified their aunt, and she piled the kids into her car and headed for Santa Barbara. We got on the phone and called other family members, who also began their journeys to the hospital.

When Todd and Taryn arrived, Taryn climbed right up on the bed and started hugging and laughing with Trevor. His face lit up and he stroked her face and hair. It was hard because she couldn't understand what he was saying.

Trevor and Todd hugged, but it was very difficult for Todd. At 10, he was much more aware of what was happening. I'll never forget him sitting on the other bed in the room crying and saying, "Why Trevor? Please not Trevor!"

I remember thinking, "This can't be happening so soon; I'm not ready yet! We haven't had enough time!" I'd tried to convince God that He needed people like Trevor here on earth. Now I thought that God's plan in letting Trevor go must be unusual because it had been so incredibly special to have him here with us for seven short years.

As family began arriving and joining us in his room, he motioned for the clipboard again. I brought it, held it for him and he was able to scribble, "Do you want to go to the sixth floor?" He knew what a peaceful place sixth floor was. Here he was—in numbing pain, his life drifting away—and he was thinking of the comfort of others. Then he formed these words to his dad: "Happy Father's Day."

The kidney stone pain began to flare up harder. We sat down in counsel with Trevor's physicians. As a nurse, I knew what was coming. If we were to medicate Trevor to a level of comfort, it would be only a matter of time and the brain stem would be depressed. It would be over. To keep him awake and in pain might mean a few more days of life for him, but for whose benefit?

Trevor had said to me a few days before, "Mommy, if I die, I don't want to die in a bad way."

When I asked him what he meant, he said, "I don't want to be choking or in pain. I just want to go to sleep." Then we'd prayed together if this were to be his journey that God would grant a peaceful experience to Trevor.

And now, because of the kidney stone I'd been so angry about, we had the opportunity to give Trevor that peaceful experience he prayed for.

Chapter Six

No More Dizziness

"As sure as ever God puts His children in the furnace, He will be in the furnace with them."
—Charles H. Spurgeon

After our counsel with the physicians—and our decision to do the merciful thing—I went in to talk with Trevor one last time. He was groggy and in pain, yet still able to nod his head and squeeze my hand. His eyes were open, watching my face.

I climbed onto the bed as I had done so many times the previous few days and held his little face close to mine. I said, "Trevie, I'm so sorry that you've had so much pain the last few days. You've been so brave; everyone is amazed at what a special boy you are. I know that you're tired, and it looks like this tumor is getting worse. We can give you some special medicine for the pain, and you'll feel better and just be able to go to sleep."

When I said the word "sleep," his eyes got big, and I knew he realized what I was saying. I asked him if that's what he wanted, and he nodded his head and squeezed my hand. I was screaming inside and couldn't say another word, so I just held him for a moment and then said "Okay, Baby, it's going to be okay." He patted my arm.

By this time many family members were present. The nurses, who had treated us like family, had arranged the nurses' lounge for our use. Family members took turns getting food and drinks for the group. Others made sure I was drinking enough water and trying to eat something. I had already lost 10 pounds in the last three weeks.

Everyone seemed to find someone to cling to and lean on during what was to be a 48-hour vigil of love and watch care over Trevor.

All monitors and life-sustaining equipment had been removed from Trevor's room. Taped instrumental praise music was playing softly. The medication was being given to Trevor regularly, and he appeared to be asleep.

His sleep could have been reversed with a narcotic antagonist drug, so he could wake up and talk with me one more time—oh please, just one more time! It had been only two hours that he had been silent, but it was already too long!

Family members took turns lying on the bed and holding Trevor. I spent most of the time lying next to him, stroking his back and hair, trying to freeze-frame what he felt like— his solid body, his little hands in mine, his perfect ears and angelic face. I continually whispered in his ear that I would always, always love him, and would see him soon when Jesus comes.

By Sunday evening, Trevor's breaths were down to just four to six per minute. His little heart was strong, and he seemed to be hanging on. Most of the family had returned to their homes to go to work the next day. My parents remained with us.

Late that night two of the nurses who had been off duty over the weekend came in to offer support to us. They rubbed our shoulders, brought us food, and cried with us. Then they asked me a startling question, "Do you want to hold your son?"

I hadn't even thought about it, but my heart melted at the opportunity. They brought in a large recliner chair, and I sat down. The nurses gently picked up Trevor's limp body and placed him in my lap. Needless to say, the floodgates opened and I sobbed from the deepest places of my soul.

I held him for about half an hour. I think he'd grown three inches since the last time he'd sat on my lap. His little heart was slowing down, but my mind was racing as I flashed on this little man's short life with us, and how extraordinary it had been. I recalled holding him in my arms as a baby, and imagining at that time what he would look like when he went to college.

My parents came into the room, and we all sang one of Trevor's favorite songs as a toddler:

Rock, rock, rock, little boat on the sparkling sea,
Rock, rock, rock, dear Jesus rides in thee,
Rock, rock, rock, o'er the waters swiftly flee,
For Jesus rides in a little boat on blue Galilee.

In those darkest hours—as I felt Trevor's life slip away—I can say that I have never in my life felt God's presence more. This was a bitter journey, yet I felt God was weeping with me, that He understood perfectly how I felt, and that there truly was a bigger picture being played out.

A Bible text came to mind, "Count it all joy when you have tribulations." And I thought, "Oh. . .sure. . .give me a break." But then I was struck with the thought that the text doesn't say *feel* it all joy. It says *count* it all joy. In other words, there are times when we may not feel joyful in our circumstances, but we can count on the fact that God is still who He is and operating from a divine plan based on mercy.

* * * * *

Monday at 5:00 a.m. it was all over. Trevor lay peaceful and quiet, and for the first time in months we could position his little head straight up and not over to his right side. There was no more dizziness!

I was numb and trying to grasp the overwhelming nature of this experience when Dr. Corazza walked into the room. He'd not been with us these last two days. We thought he'd left on a family vacation. But something had delayed his plans, and he'd been notified of Trevor's death.

The doctor came around the bedside to us, and we all stood in silence for a few moments. With tears in his eyes, he expressed his sorrow to us. Then he pulled a tiny New Testament from his back pocket. He said, "I don't often get to do this with parents because they wouldn't be comfortable. But because we've shared a common faith and hope, I wanted to share this with you. He began to read:

"I consider that our present sufferings are not worth comparing with the glory that will be revealed in us. . .

"And we know that in all things God works for the good of those who love Him, who have been called according to His purpose. . .

"What, then, shall we say in response to this? If God is for us, who can be against us? He who did not spare His own Son, but gave Him up for us all—how will He not also, along with Him, graciously give us all things?. . .

"Who shall separate us from the love of Christ? Shall trouble or hardship or persecution or famine or nakedness or danger or sword?. . .

"No, in all these things we are more than conquerors through Him who loved us. For I am

convinced that neither death nor life, neither angels nor demons, neither the present nor the future, nor any powers, neither height nor depth, nor anything else in all creation, will be able to separate us from the love of God that is in Christ Jesus our Lord."
—*Romans 8:18, 28-32, 35, 37-38, NIV*

And through the fog of numbness and pain I heard these familiar words and knew that I believed them. But I wasn't able to celebrate them, not now.

Yet in my soul I knew there was power in these words and that by repeating them we had spit in the face of the presence of evil in this world—so much that is evil and unfair, so much that is painful.

I knew that a victory had been won here. A little soul was safe and no longer touchable by the powers of darkness in this world. It would just take time to be willing to accept the comfort that these words could bring.

As I looked at Trevor's now-paling face and kissed his quickly cooling forehead, I was inspired with a comforting concept. Jeremiah 1:5 *NIV* says:

> *"Before I formed you in the womb I knew you,*
> *before you were born I set you apart."*

I believe what the Bible teaches about death—it is a sleep; and that while the breath and spirit return to God who gave it, "the dead know not anything." Ecclesiastes 9:5, *KJV*

For it's breath from God that makes a living soul. There's something about the essence of who we really are that is not about what we see or touch. What is most real about us is our spirit—and that is always with God.

If you and I have always been a thought in the mind of God—and if there is that part of us that has always been with God, and returns to Him when our breathing stops— then if God dwells in my heart, Trevor and I are always connected to each other. We're never separated from the love we have with each other. In this way Trevor will be with me always.

Trevor sleeps now—and his next waking thoughts will be resurrection morning! No passing of time for him!

And on the darkest morning of my life I clung to the brightest hope of *that* morning.

Chapter Seven

The Next Indicated Thing

"You hurled me into the deep, into the very heart
of the seas, and the currents swirled about me;
all your waves and breakers swept over me.
I said, 'I have been banished from your sight;
yet I will look again toward your holy temple.'
The engulfing waters threatened me, the deep
surrounded me; seaweed was wrapped around my
head. To the roots of the mountains I sank down;
the earth beneath barred me in forever. But you
brought my life up from the pit, O Lord my God."
—*Jonah 2:3-6, NIV*

With all that happened, some of the most difficult
moments were those immediately following Trevor's death.
To be gathering up his things while his little body lay still
and quiet on the bed was surreal.

Yet I didn't want the nurses to place a sheet over him
until I left. It would feel like I was trying to forget already—
to distance myself from the experience.

My greatest fear then (which continues to this day) was
that I'd forget. I wanted to remember everything. I'd come
to realize in those last two weeks that the pain was part of
the loving. They go together; they are not mutually exclu-
sive. If you shut out the pain, you also shut out the love and
joy. To love someone deeply carries with it the constant

threat of deep loss and pain. The extent that we love will be the extent that we feel pain. The pain was my connectedness to my endless love for Trevor.

I could still hear his slurred speech as he said "Bye, bye" to his broccoli before eating it. I could see his dancing smile, even in the struggle. I felt his little arms around my neck and his lips against mine.

I knew that the body that remained wasn't the real Trevor. He was sleeping now, yet everything inside me wanted to stay beside him. I thought of *National Geographic* videos I'd seen where animal mothers would sit for days beside their dead babies before moving on with their herd.

I didn't want to go. The last 15 days of Trevor's life with us were spent there. But of course I had to go. Life is to be lived as long as we have breath.

I walked outside the hospital and looked up to his room, which faced the entrance. I'd glanced at it every time I came and went for the past 15 days. This time was the last. A little body was up there. A little body that had come out of my own just seven short years before. I was only beginning to realize what a blessing that short life had been.

Then I was getting into the car and driving away. . . driving away. . .

Walking back into our house was the next hurdle. I knew as I opened the front door that I was leaving a phase of my life that—until now—had been untouched by deep sorrow. I was entering into a new phase of enormous and sobering challenge. I hadn't been in the house much since those three weeks of having Trevor home.

I sat down in the living room. Almost everything was back to normal. The hospital bed had been removed, with the overhead trapeze with which Trevor had tried to do pull-ups. But the poster on the wall was still there, where we'd listed a schedule for him of exercises and rest periods every hour of every day. On the poster were many stars for efforts well done. Was he really here only two weeks ago, trying to build his strength and rehabilitate?

I looked for him to round a corner, and give me a hearty hug as usual. I looked for him everywhere. . .

I searched my mind for options to escape the pain I knew lay ahead. I knew there was no going around this. I would have to go *through*. In the deepest places of my soul I saw myself moving forward, but I was already feeling the rising tide of grief—and it was filling every crack and crevice of my spirit.

I sensed clearly the choices in front of me about the direction my life would now take. In my feeble, fumbling exhaustion, I decided to lean into it as my friend Karen had suggested some weeks before.

As Gerald Sittser was struggling with the loss of three loved ones at once, his sister, Diane, said to him, ". . .the quickest way for anyone to reach the sun and the light of day is not to run west, chasing after the setting sun, but to head east, plunging into the darkness until one comes to the sunrise."[1]

I chose the mysterious process of being healed through suffering, even though I didn't fully know what that meant. In his book *Disappointment with God*, Philip Yancey says "The alternative to disappointment *with* God seems to be disappointment *without* God."[2] [emphasis supplied]

Coming home was such a letdown for us all. There had been clarity in the required functions during the critical closing days of Trevor's life. All our energies were focused and poised. Now we seemed to stumble over each other, not knowing what to do next.

I went through the motions and did the next indicated thing. I felt like I was having an out-of-body experience. The real me was locked up and could come out only for brief moments at a time because of the sting that any feelings at all would inflict on such a fresh wound.

Besides the ongoing daily requirements of home life, we were faced with going to the funeral home the next day to discuss burial plans and walking out to the cemetery and seeing the little plot. Planning a burial and a memorial service are things you think your kids will have to do for *you* someday—as a parent, you don't expect to do them for your *child.*

Two days later our immediate families gathered for a private graveside ceremony. It was in this same cemetery that Trevor had learned to ride a bike just two years before. Who could have anticipated that he would be buried there on a peaceful day in June?

But there we were, about 25 of us, a congregation clinging to each other as we stood around the little mound of dirt. We were solemn, as each one remembered this special life that was so acutely missed already. I thought of the words we'd selected for his tombstone, "Precious son, how you inspired us. Sleep now, and soon Jesus will call you, and we will never part again."

We sang the song "It Is Well with My Soul." It held special meaning for me because it was written by Horatio Spafford, who sent for his wife and four children to visit him in Europe. Six days after they left New York harbor their ship collided with a sailing vessel. When the ship sank, all the passengers were thrown into the water. Mrs. Spafford was separated from her children. Later she was taken out of the water unconscious, but her children were all lost.

From Wales she cabled her husband: "Saved alone."

On receiving the unspeakable news, Attorney Spafford wrote this hymn:

When peace, like a river, attendeth my way,
When sorrows like sea billows roll—
Whatever my lot, Thou hast taught me to say,
It is well, it is well with my soul.

And, Lord, haste the day when my faith shall be sight,
The clouds be rolled back as a scroll:
The trump shall resound and the Lord shall descend,
"Even so"—it is well with my soul.

My father officiated at that sweet ceremony. He began by validating our feelings of confusion, shock, anger, and exhaustion. He reviewed Trevor's life and how dear he was to us all. He reflected on the ordeal of the past few weeks and of the soul-searching we'd all been doing. He quoted verses that I'd memorized as a child, but now were glaringly clear and full of meaning to me:

"We are hard pressed on every side, but not crushed; perplexed, but not in despair; persecuted, but not abandoned; struck down, but not destroyed. . .Therefore we do not lose heart. Though outwardly we are wasting away, yet inwardly we are being renewed day by day. For our light and momentary troubles are achieving for us an eternal glory that far outweighs them all. So we fix our eyes. . . on what is unseen. For what is seen is temporary, but what is unseen is eternal."
—2 Corinthians 4:8, 9, 16-18, NIV

Then he asked the question, "Is it too soon to celebrate?"
What might seem like a cruel and cold question began to warm me inside as we reaffirmed the truth about God's sovereignty. We reviewed His all-knowing and all-loving nature, His unchanging character, His promise of an imminent return, and the reunions that we'll celebrate throughout eternity. *Death, then, does not have the final word—God does!* Someday this little mound of dirt will rumble and split open, and Christ Himself will call forth our dear red-headed boy from his dusty grave.

It's *not* too soon to celebrate that reunion! Trevor had

often said, "The next voice I hear will be Jesus telling me, 'Trevor, wake up, it's time to go home!'"

That vision and hope sustains me to this day. The phrase "homesick for heaven" has never had such meaning for me as it does now. I yearn for it.

The next day we had the memorial service at our church in Arroyo Grande. I had a hundred different emotions going through me—yet at the same time I was detached from them. Trevor had loved being in this church. He'd loved singing songs. He'd loved it when Miss Ruth told the children's story and all the kids went to the steps by the platform. He'd wave to me from his spot at the front of the sanctuary.

Sometimes after everyone had filed out of the church, he'd go up front and grab the microphone (which was off by this time), and pretend to be singing or preaching. Today the singing and preaching were *about* Trevor.

Until Trevor's memorial service, my experience with "standing-room-only" attendance at church was limited. Now more than 500 people crowded the sanctuary. Some had traveled six hours to attend. Some I had not seen in years. Some I had never even met.

Looking into the faces of family and friends I realized that they, too, were suffering the loss of Trevor. Each one had a different relationship to him. They had lost a friend, a play-mate, a cousin, a nephew, a grandchild, a student. My heart went out to them, as I saw that they hurt, too. I was reminded that each person is many different things to many different people.

We had community in our woundedness. Even people who had not personally known Trevor were overcome with grief as they heard the remembrances of him and observed our pain.

Many of Trevor's teachers and friends shared their fond-est memories and moments when Trevor had touched their lives. His classmates sang some of his favorite songs. One of the dear women in the church who had come with her husband frequently to the hospital to visit Trevor and bring him M & Ms, wrote a poem for him.

We came together to mourn and grieve, but more importantly to celebrate a life lived to the fullest. We joined in celebrating the love that bound us together and the hope we have of seeing Trevor again, when God shall wipe away all tears and make all things new.

And yet, while all of this proper perspective was being affirmed amongst us, I felt as if life had stopped for me. Flowers were colorless, the air was thick as a fog, and even the music, which usually wakes up my spirit, seemed to have only one monotonous note. And then the memorial service was over.

But life continued for all of us. It was June, and there were new leaves on the trees, new flowers, new baby creatures happy to be alive. The bills kept coming, people still got up and went to work, still took vacations at Disneyland, still bought ice cream cones. I was beginning to live a tremendous tension—mourning and living simultaneously.

When I tried to pray I felt paralyzed. I'd prayed my heart out when Trevor was alive—and now I felt let down. I knew I fundamentally trusted God's dealings with me, but felt so disappointed. I even began to ask God to pray for me.

"I don't know what to say, Lord, and I don't know what I need most right now, so You pray for me. You've bought me with a price, and I'm your responsibility." As I began to talk to God in this fashion, I was led to do two things.

First, to be completely real and honest with God about my feelings—my fears, my confusion, my anger, my deep sorrow. Second, to be still and listen.

I began to notice that if I began my major grief seasons by thinking about the life I *wasn't* going to have with Trevor— and all the things I was missing—I'd end the session feeling angry and sorry for myself. But if I began the session with prayer, asking God to hold me and reveal Himself to me, although I did not get answers, I did receive peace and comfort. I felt His presence with me, and I would usually end the session looking at Trevor's pictures, laughing aloud and feeling grateful that he was in my life at all.

Being still and listening is so important. So often our prayers are full of requests or praise, which are appropriate, but I think God longs to communicate with us.

And with our finite, thick skulls, it takes some time to get through! We have to create the posture of readiness to receive His messages.

As I came out of these surrendered grief times, I realized I needed a new definition of the word "miracle." While we prayed for a physical healing miracle for Trevor, miracles were happening all around us. Here are some of the miracles I came to understand:

First was the healing of hearts as people rallied around us to offer practical, *real* help. That much-appreciated help came as money, food (at one point three truckloads of food were delivered to our home, and 33 boxes of cereal were stacked in the garage!), a homemade dinner delivered every night for a month, as well as help with errands and cleaning. Truly people are God's hands extended, and I felt His love and comfort in the hugs and helping hands of so many. That God chooses to love through *us* is a real miracle.

More profound was the miracle of revival that took place in many hearts as believers struggled with God about the issues of pain and suffering. The one who approaches God with the intent of discovering His purposes will not come away the same. God's answer to Job's agonizing questions was to reveal Himself. I came to realize the truth in what Gerald Sittser had written:

"…Job stopped asking questions not because God was a bully, but because Job finally beheld God's unfathom-

*able greatness in his immediate experience. He had spoken **about** God; then he came to **know** God. On meeting the real God, he simply had no more questions to ask. He discovered that God is the answer to all his questions, even questions he had not thought to ask."[3]*
[emphasis supplied]

How interesting it is that we decide ahead of time just what miracle it is that we will recognize, and what answer to prayer it is that we will acknowledge and accept. I came to believe there were many answers to our prayers; these are the ones that now mean the most to me:

- The gift of time. Although we had only two short weeks together with Trevor once we knew the diagnosis, we were able to say what we wanted to say and love in ways we might not have in a long lifetime together. We were able to have closure.

- The answer to the prayer for a peaceful and merciful sleep made possible because of the blessing of the kidney stone.

- And now the many opportunities that have come to me to share this story with others. They, in turn, have shared their stories with me and we have embraced each other—and learned from each other in mutual brokenness.

A few months after Trevor died a client was in my office. She saw the pictures I have of my three children and the conversation moved briefly to the experience with Trevor. She said to me, "My little 2-year-old Josh died of pneumonia last year. I prayed for a physical healing for him, but *God chose to heal me instead!*" A sermon was preached in that touching testimony. We embraced each other in a shared understanding that I would not have been able to have with her the year before.

A few months after our ordeal I was asked to do an interview with the *Voice of Prophecy* radio broadcast regarding Trevor's journey. After the program aired, a pastor from Georgia called me and said, "I heard your testimony about your experience with your son. I wonder if you'd be willing to tell me more, or share your notes with me. I'd like to preach a sermon about Trevor for my Easter Sunday service. I have a membership of 500, and a lot of hurting people, and I want them to hear your message." It was a heart-warming feeling on Easter Sunday to know that somewhere in Georgia 500 people were hearing Trevor's story about the unending trustworthiness of God in painful times.

After I'd spoken briefly at a Christian women's retreat, one woman wrote to me and said, "I know you prayed for a healing for your son, but to me, the greatest evidence of God's healing power is in your *response*, and the drawing of *my* heart to Him."

I was beginning to see this "greater good" emerge—a good that I'd sworn to God was not possible. That one small child could affect so many lives—some that he didn't even know—was evidence that the Holy Spirit was in this, with every intention of turning a tragedy into triumph. That signed, blank page that I'd finally given to God was beginning to fill up, and I had a feeling there would be entries into it that would go on through eternity.

But I still had much wrestling to do. As time went by and the "survival mode" began to subside, I realized that this ache in my gut would never go away. There were so many unanswered questions, and I began to hunger for a blanket of peace to wrap around me and keep me from the biting sting of sadness.

Help Me
I Need To Understand

Section Two

Under His wings I am safely abiding;
Though the night deepens and tempests are wild,
Still I can trust Him; I know He will keep me;
He has redeemed me, and I am His child.

Under His wings, what a refuge in sorrow!
How the heart yearningly turns to its rest!
Often when earth has no balm for my healing,
There I find comfort, and there I am blest.

Under His wings, O what precious enjoyment!
There will I hide till life's trials are o'er;
Sheltered, protected, no evil can harm me;
Resting in Jesus I'm safe evermore.

Refrain:
Under His wings, under His wings,
Who from His love can sever?
Under His wings my soul shall abide,
Safely abide forever.

Chapter Eight

The Real Questions

> **"Some people complain because God puts thorns on roses, while others praise Him for putting roses among thorns."**
> —Author unknown

> **"God has a thousand ways**
> **Where I cannot see one.**
> **When all my means have reached an end**
> **Then His have just begun."**
> —Esther Guyot

In those first few weeks after Trevor died everyday activities became painful reminders of the subtraction that had taken place in our family: having more room in the car; setting the table for four instead of five; calling the children and having to leave out Trevor; signing cards and having to leave off Trevor's name; shopping for school clothes for Todd, and seeing shirts and pants Trevor would have wanted. I found myself saying Trevor's name aloud frequently, and writing his name to myself, just to keep him with me.

One day while shopping I saw a shirt exactly like the one Trevor had worn as often as he could. I began to cry. When a young saleswoman came over, I explained my tears. She sat down on the floor with me and we shed tears together.

For some reason folding laundry was a difficult time for me. The last few months of Trevor's life, it had been getting harder to tell Todd's and Trevor's clothes apart, especially the socks and underwear. Now it was painfully easy. Only one boy in the family now. . .

After six months or so the shock began to wear off, and I knew *emotionally* that Trevor was never coming back. I realized that I had to settle into the "living with it."

Have you ever experienced something, then suddenly noticed others experiencing the same thing? It's fascinating that often we're not aware of other's experiences until we're experiencing the same thing. For example, when I was pregnant with Todd, it seemed there was an epidemic of pregnant women in my town. I noticed them everywhere! I wondered if there was "something in the water."

On another occasion I'd torn ligaments in my ankle, and was in a cast for a few weeks. Wouldn't you know it, several other people in my town had the same misfortune. Suddenly it seemed like the "in" thing to be sporting a cast.

And now that I was weighed down with grief, sure enough, there seemed to be grieving people all around me. Had they been there all the time? I noticed I was much more sensitive to tragedies in the news and needed not only to be settled about my own loss, but also to be settled about pain I saw the world over. I began to study about suffering and loss.

I believe God led—and continues to lead—me to the written and spoken words of others. The bibliography at the end of this book lists those sources I've found most helpful. I've learned so much from this shared testimony. This is a lifetime journey and no one has "arrived." My prayer is that as I share with you some of what I'm learning it will help you to "pack your bag" for your own journey.

We're acutely aware of the maddening world around us. Every time we see or hear the news we're bombarded with the atrocities of life. With every breath we take, someone, somewhere is experiencing a new wave of loss or change.

Looking at the world around us does not help us to

understand God. Lawrence Crabb states it so well:

> *"No one will conclude God is good by studying life. . . . If left to our own way of thinking, every one of us would conclude that God either is bad, or doesn't exist, that no God in this universe is good enough to be trusted with the things that matter most. We may ask Him to bless our food, but we won't trust Him when a loved one betrays us. As we look at how God treats some of His children, even those who abandon themselves fully to His care, we're not impressed."[1]*

How desperately we want life to be fair, yet loss is not a respecter of persons. Some people seem to live in health and wealth and happiness all their lives. Others seem to experience one heartache after another. We might think that those who hurt others deserve to suffer loss, and that those who've lived a life of benevolence deserve to be blessed.

But we have only to look around us to see that people do not suffer or prosper on the basis of their merits. People don't always get what they deserve. If I say that I didn't deserve to lose Trevor, then the truth is I didn't deserve his precious presence in my life either. Gradually I came to believe as Gerald Sittser wrote:

> *"...I would prefer to take my chances living in a universe in which I get what I do not deserve. . . either way. That means that I will suffer loss, as I already have, but it also means I will receive mercy. Life will end up being far worse than it would have otherwise been; it will also end up being far better. . . I dread experiencing undeserved pain, but it is worth it to me if I can also experience undeserved grace."[2]*

For me, the most difficult aspect of the whole issue is the seeming randomness of suffering. As a nurse I've had to deal for years with the suffering that comes from illness, so maybe it's a little less tormenting for me to accept.

As I was working on this chapter, I heard a news report of a young woman and her 3-year-old daughter who were sitting in their living room watching television. Two stray bullets from a semiautomatic, fired hundreds of feet away, sailed into that room and ended both of their lives instantly.

Yesterday a family from the midwest was sightseeing along the coast of California. They'd never been around the ocean and didn't know the dangers of the currents along this shore. The 10-year-old wanted to get wet, so she climbed down the rocks and dipped into the water. Her horrified family watched as she was swept under the waves. In an attempt to rescue her, the mother also entered the water and began to struggle with the current. Then the grandmother went in to try to help the mother. All three lives were lost. The little brother stood on the bank, observing it all.

And the examples of tragedy march on. A family lives in a house for 30 years and one day a tornado rips through their town, devouring their house and leaving the rest on the block standing. A middle-aged man who has eaten right and exercised regularly goes to the doctor for strange abdominal pains, is diagnosed with pancreatic cancer, and given four months to live. A young father forgets for the first time to latch the gate of the fence around the swimming pool, and his 2-year-old son wanders in and drowns.

These are not stories created for a full-length feature film. These are the devastating and disturbing stories we listen to everyday on the news. Combine these with the inhumane slaughtering and starvation occurring all over the world, and it makes a person want to scream.

We have a tendency to blame God for it. After all, if He has the power to stop it, why *doesn't* He? Ah, the crippling "Why" question! This simple word, when asked enough, can freeze you where you stand. We seem to want God to shatter the evil around us with one stupendous act of mercy!

As Philip Yancey says:

> *"Some people stake all their faith on a miracle, as if a miracle would eliminate all disappointment with God. It wouldn't. . . .Something is still badly wrong with this planet . . .all of us die. The ultimate mortality rate is the same for atheists and saints alike."*[3]

In most of the books I've read on suffering, the story of Job is discussed. Like stagehands, we get to peek in on what's going on behind the scene. Since the beginning of time, Satan has accused God of being untrustworthy, and he presents Job as a shining example of someone who serves God because he's been blessed with so much health and wealth. The entire universe is watching, and heavenly hosts of angels are observing this drama being played out. God permits Satan to enact his devastation on Job.

Our modern minds don't like to accept God's refusal to answer Job's questions. We're so used to touching the evidence, to having computer printouts that prove our point. We cannot imagine a world without answers, so we continue to bombard God. The most frequently asked question by one who suffers, is *Why?* or *Why me?* or *Why now?*

Think about that last one for a moment. If we were really in control of our lives, would we ever choose a time when it was "okay" to suffer a tragic loss?

Isn't it interesting that we don't tend to ask *Why?* or *Why me?* when good things are coming our way? It seems rather arrogant that we would see nothing unusual or unexpected about receiving easy times, yet rear our heads in shock and dismay when hard times hit.

Philip Yancey's book *Disappointment with God* has had the most profound effect on my healing. I've come to share his belief when he discusses the *why* questions, "Perhaps God keeps us ignorant because we are incapable of comprehending the answer."[4]

Personal experiences during my nursing career—especially being with scores of families in turmoil—helped prepare me for my own worse tragedy. I found myself asking *Why not me?* I came to realize this response acknowledges that suffering is a part of life, a universal experience.

Now that I've endured a great loss, can I count on having met my earthly quota for heartache? Am I guaranteed not to experience more loss; that my other children will outlive me; that I'll remain in good physical health? Of course not!

Loss takes away our sense of control. We come face to face with our own limitations, but we *can choose* to look from a different perspective. I love this little verse by an unknown author. It shows that cancer—one of the most feared of all diseases—cannot take away the most precious things of this life:

Cancer is limited.
It cannot cripple love; It cannot erode faith;
It cannot eat away peace; It cannot destroy confidence;
It cannot kill friendship; It cannot shut out memories;
It cannot silence courage; It cannot invade the soul;
It cannot reduce eternal life; It cannot quench the spirit;
It cannot lessen the power of the resurrection!

What really matters can never be destroyed! But most of us don't live trusting in that reality. We're feverishly focused on the *becoming* and not on the *being*, and we never really experience the gifts found in *what is*.

As I pondered these issues, I began to sense that answers could not be found; that I was now part of this collective, inevitable experience we call suffering. I needed to reflect more honestly on my view of God because now I realized everything depended on who I believed Him to be.

Chapter Nine

Our Benevolent Butler?

". . .His compassions fail not.
They are new every morning:
great is thy faithfulness."
—Lamentations 3:22-23, KJV

"This, this is the God we adore
Our faithful, unchangeable friend,
Whose love is as great as his power,
And neither knows measure nor end."
—Joseph Hart

In our culture we have a passion for the relief of pain. At the first sign of discomfort we're programmed to run for relief rather than listen and learn.

We can comprehend the concept that pain is meant to alert us—to direct our attention to a physical state that's out of balance. Yet most of us quickly go for a substance or prescribed remedy that will make us feel comfortable again. Sometimes taking over-the-counter medications masks the true nature of the pain and makes it more difficult for the physician to assess and diagnose the problem.

Pain is a built-in alarm and protection, one of the highest functions of our bodies. Dr. Paul Brand has recounted his years of work with Hansen's disease (previously known as leprosy) in his book *The Gift of Pain.* Those with Hansen's disease constantly risk injuring themselves because they don't have pain sensors intact. He tells stories of people harming themselves because they're completely unaware of pain.

I might be able to convince you of the necessity of physical pain. But what about the necessity of emotional or spiritual pain? If physical pain is meant to alert us to our physical condition, is not emotional or spiritual pain meant to alert us to our emotional and spiritual condition?

I've worked with hundreds of patients with diabetes. And I've survived and moved beyond my own eating disorder. From these experiences I can testify that most of us try to "fix" an emotional or spiritual pain with a physical remedy, such as food, alcohol or drugs. Or we escape into overachieving, or doing nothing, or even obsession with religion. Anything outside ourselves that we *use* to numb feelings of sadness, woundedness, anger, loneliness, guilt, or fear only addicts us to that substance, activity, or person.

Gradually I came to understand that we need to understand that pain and joy can exist together—that they are part of the same wonderful design. The pain of loss is excruciating because the joy of life is exhilarating.

I'm intrigued by my own response to pain, especially the pain of loss—the pain that fills me with so many questions and, yes, even doubts. Few discussions on this matter have hit home for me as directly as the thoughts of Lawrence Crabb in his book *Finding God*.

He speaks of how we are more passionate about relieving the pain of our problems than using that pain to wrestle with the purposes of God; that we are more desiring of the satisfaction He can give than of experiencing Him directly. I saw myself in his explanation of how we treat God as a divine butler, as if He exists for our service, so that on that great reunion day in heaven we can say to the Lord, "Well done, Lord, you have served us well."

My struggle has been to find a spot that seems trouble-free, a point in time when I've "gotten over" the frustrations and disappointments of life. And I admit as a Christian I subconsciously believed that God would take extra notice of me, of my worthwhile efforts for His cause, and that would "line me up" and entitle me to His relief of my problems.

But I found myself continually disappointed and let down. Now in my mid-forties, I find myself seeing for the first time what life really is, and more importantly, seeing God for who *He* really is.

I'm beginning to find a greater capacity to love because I'm no longer consumed with being *satisfied*. I understand now that God never promised ultimate relief and contentment here. *Rather we were promised His presence and power to live in this imperfect world and maintain unwavering confidence in the One who can equip us—while keeping our eyes fixed on that better day that is coming.*

The ache we feel in our gut is homesickness for heaven, where we *will* experience the ultimate contentment and live in the perfect presence of our Lord whom *we* have served well, regardless of our earthly circumstances.

Who is this God who's more desirous of my trust than my total satisfaction? My response to Him has everything to do with my image of Him. In his book *When Life is Changed Forever*, Rick Taylor discusses four different views of God.

The first is *God as Godfather*. He pulls all the right strings and is powerfully committed to those who are loyal to Him, but He can turn in a moment from commitment to cruelty. If we have this view of God, we'll struggle always to be on His good side, and cower from His anger if we make a mistake. If a disappointment or tragedy comes along, we'll believe that we've done something to arouse God's displeasure.

The second harmful view is *God as Superman*. He is very powerful and all His motives are pure. He wants to spare us from suffering, but He does have limitations. He's sort of a willing, but unable, hero. To us, this God is not powerful enough, and we feel let down.

The third picture is *God as Heavenly Scorekeeper.* In this role He's powerful, but has chosen to be distant from our lives. He's pulled back to keep score. There's no chance for personal relationship with this God, and when life is over, He just adds up the score and gives us what we deserve. In times of loss, this is not a God we can go to, and all of our good "points" don't seem to mean much. The prospect of living throughout eternity in the presence of this kind of God is at best depressing.

Lastly, Taylor offers *God as Genie in a Bottle.* This God will do anything, at any time we ask. All you have to do is "rub the bottle" by praying enough—and He appears to grant our wishes. He's under our control and exists to please us.

Consider for a moment the kind of world where God did exactly as we demanded. We'd live for centuries, never have illness or catastrophe. Our businesses would all be success-ful, our houses beautiful, our cars the newest and best. People would seek God in order to get the "goods" rather than respond from hearts of love. We wouldn't need faith. *But* when faced with death, we'd call on Him to keep it from happening, and when there was no response, we'd feel aban-doned and rejected. Alone.

Two texts in Scripture helped me to come to terms with a God whose ways I could not fathom.

> *"As you do not know the path of the wind, or how*
> *the body is formed in a mother's womb, so you cannot*
> *understand the work of God, the Maker of all things."*
> *—Ecclesiastes 11:5, NIV*

> *"For my thoughts are not your thoughts, neither are*
> *your ways my ways. . . As the heavens are higher than*
> *the earth, so are my ways higher than your ways and*
> *my thoughts than your thoughts."*
> *—Isaiah 55:8-9, NIV*

Isn't it a relief not to have the responsibility of trying to figure out God? My struggle and yours is simple. We must trust Him to be who He says He is, to be Lord of our life, whether the present evidence is clear or not.

I began to search Scripture to find out more about God. Look at the myriad names in the Bible that are attributed to God, and describe His character:

- Counselor
- The Vine
- Bread of Life
- Refuge
- Creator
- Lily of the Valley
- Everlasting Father
- The Great "I Am"
- Light of the World
- The Morning Star
- Mighty God
- Prince of Peace
- Good Shepherd
- King of Kings
- Our Father
- The Resurrection and the Life
- Lord of Lords
- The Way, the Truth, and the Life
- The Almighty
- Lion of the Tribe of Judah
- Alpha and Omega

To me these characteristics don't seem consistent with descriptions of God as a Godfather, Superman, Heavenly Scorekeeper, or the Genie in the Bottle. So I decided to look further at the life of our Lord.

Jesus Christ came to reveal God as He wanted to be known. The Bible says,

> *"He was in the world, and though the world was made through him, the world did not recognize him. He came to that which was his own, but his own did not receive him. Yet to all who received him, to those who believed in his name, he gave the right to become children of God."*
>
> *—John 1:10-12, NIV*

Before Christ came to this earth, God's faithful children had been long awaiting His coming as Messiah. But when He finally did come, they didn't recognize Him because He did not bring the type of relief they wanted. They wanted relief from oppression, from debt, from pain.

He wanted to establish His kingdom in their hearts and empower them to live *in* the world—a world which was to remain unfair, cruel, and punishing. His unconditional love was meant to transform them into healers of souls, and those who accepted His spiritual kingdom did not experience less pain or suffering. In fact, many endured far more.

But they possessed a steeliness about what really mattered, a passion to love others unconditionally, and an ache for the fulfilled promise of a day when He would "come back and take you to be with me that you also may be where I am." (John 14:3b, *NIV*)

To reveal God's desire for restoration Christ practiced healing, but on the day He healed some, others still died. And all of those He healed eventually died, some other way, some other day. Evidently when He said, "I have come that they may have life, and have it to the full" (John 10:10b, *NIV*) he was talking about something *other* than abundant physical health and wealth.

Finally, at the cross the question "What is God like?" was answered for all eternity. Christ revealed a God who operates from a basis of love, rather than a basis of power; a God who chooses to woo us instead of wow us; a God who is forever for us and with us. As Philip Yancey says so poignantly:

> *"The deepest longings we feel on earth, as parents, as lovers, are mere flickers of the hungering desire God feels for us."*[1]

Once my fuzzy picture of God popped into focus, I was ready to take another look at my own expectations of life.

Chapter Ten

A Matter of Expectations

> "It is not because things are good that we are to thank the Lord, but because He is good. We are not wise enough to judge as to things, whether they are really joys or sorrows. But we always know the Lord is good, and everything He provides or permits must be good."
> —*Hannah Whitall Smith*

It's an interesting phenomenon, this shock and surprise when disaster strikes, as if we Christians were somehow immune to such things.

We sing the Doxology to open our worship services: "Praise God from whom all blessings flow." We define blessings as any good thing that happens or agrees with our agendas. When we don't receive blessings according to how hard we've tried—or worse yet, when the storms come even when we've really been trying—we become disillusioned. Life, and ultimately God, isn't measuring up to our expectations.

The direction we choose to go in life has everything to do with what we anticipate life holding for us. James Dobson says it concisely:

> "*. . .contentment in life is determined, in part, by what a person anticipates from it. To a man. . .who thought he would soon die quickly, everything takes on*

*meaning. . .those who believe life owes them a free ride
are often discontent with its finest gifts."[1]*

I decided I needed to take a closer look at what I
anticipated in life. I looked up the word *expectation* in the
dictionary and a thesaurus and found these synonyms—
hope, belief, prospect, counted upon, relied upon, foreseen,
predictable, prepared for, budgeted for, within normal
expectations. I tried writing down a series of statements that
I'd never before contemplated:

> — I anticipate suffering in my life.
> — I'm counting on suffering in my life.
> — I'm budgeted for suffering in my life.
> — I'm prepared for suffering in my life.
> — Suffering will not take me by surprise because
>   I can rely on the fact that it comes to all.

How do these statements feel? Maybe if we expected
difficult times, our term for such seasons would not be
suffering. When you see these statements, the issue of *why*
becomes less important. What emerges as critical is *How?
How am I preparing? How will I respond?*

It's normal to wonder how you'll respond to an
unexpected situation. When I was in nurses' training, we
were only allowed to stand in the door and observe a Code
Blue resuscitation effort. When I graduated and began work
in an intensive-care unit, I fearfully anticipated the inevitable first time I'd have to function in such a crisis.

I used my 20-minute drive to work every morning to
review what I'd do when the Code Blue happened. I'd taken
a course in Advanced Life Support, so I went over and over
in my mind the protocols and procedures that would be
involved. I also envisioned myself in the patient's room,
reacting purposefully and calmly, not losing my cool.

Three months later the inevitable *did* occur, and a patient in our unit suffered cardiac arrest. Although my heart was racing, I'll never forget the feeling that I'd been there before. It was clear what I needed to do. That response, I'm sure, was largely because of my intense mental preparation.

How often do we actually contemplate what our response will be in a crisis? What will you do—more importantly, what will your attitude be—if a parent dies, if your house is destroyed by fire, if you lose your job? Should we think of these things all the time, expecting the sky to fall? No! However, if we give thought to potential misfortunes, we're more likely to equip ourselves with the attitudes and armament necessary to "stack the odds" for a less devastating outcome.

If you believe that "normal life" means only "painless opportunity," then the challenges of life will not be expected. They will be "unfair intrusions" into what is supposed to be your unfettered existence. But when you accept that the rain is needed for the rainbow, that the tough times are also "normal" times, then you will expect the struggles and be more likely to position yourself to see events from God's perspective—as having eternal meaning and purpose.

Positioning yourself involves planning ahead and being prepared for the tough times. It requires the building of a ship that can withstand the stormy seas.

For a sailboat to maintain a steady course, not capsize, and harness the power of the wind, there must be more weight below the waterline than above it. You can have fancy riggings, polished brass fittings, oak decking, and the most sophisticated nautical equipment available—but when the storm comes, your boat will remain steady or sink based on what's below the waterline.

In *The Life God Blesses*, George McDonald describes this weight below the waterline as our souls. Just as with boats, most of our efforts go into the appearances and adequacies *above* the waterline, where life is seen. But the true strength of spirit lies in what's *below* the waterline, the unseen part.

We're masters at manipulating and rearranging the upper deck, but only God can develop weight and balance where it's really needed. Only God can nurture, feed, and grow our souls. As Lawrence Crabb says, "Finding God in this life does not mean building a house in a land of no storms; rather, it means building a house that no storm can destroy."[2]

With these thoughts in mind, I decided to rewrite my life beliefs and expectations. Now they look like this:

— I believe God's greatest desire is for a love relationship with me, one built on trust and faith, and He will not withhold anything from me that will serve to draw us closer together.

— I believe God's ability to carry me is not based on my ability to hold on.

— I believe I can hold my Heavenly Father accountable for the course He's charted for my life, and someday, when I see Him face to face, that course will make perfect sense.

— I believe my God is carrying me at this moment.

— I expect to have difficult times in my life.

— I expect those around me will never be able to perfectly meet my needs.

— I expect God will seem silent and distant at times.

— I expect that I will not always feel joyful.

— I expect that I will not always feel in pain.

— I expect that to the extent I embrace my pain—to that same extent I will experience joy.

As I think back to my life before Trevor died, I realize that I thought tragedies happened to *others*. My unexpressed expectation was that I'd get what I thought I deserved.

Suddenly, a terrible storm struck—my precious son died, despite our best efforts to save him. I felt let down by God, as if He were supposed to protect me from all pain.

Now I'm learning that life on this earth is about sunshine and rain. What's most important is how I choose to respond when those raindrops spatter down.

Chapter Eleven

Where Are We When It Hurts?

"It is but right that our hearts should be on God, when the heart of God is so much on us."
—Richard Baxter

"Don't try to hold God's hand; let Him hold yours. Let Him do the holding and you the trusting."
—Hammer William Webb-Peploe

Where is God when it hurts?

How often I uttered that question after Trevor died! And I've heard it cried by many others. The question is born out of the silence that we so often experience—that time when God is quiet. I wanted a blimp to fly overhead trailing the answers, but there was none.

In *My Utmost for His Highest*, Oswald Chambers states that when God is the most silent, that's the time when He's being the most intimate with us. The most intimate human relationships are comfortable with silence; it's in silence that souls connect. That level of intimacy with God can't happen without contact, experienced most effectively in silence. So when He seems absent, He may be the closest of all.

Christ himself felt forsaken by God. He felt the apparent hiddenness of God when He cried out from the cross in the last few moments of His life, "My God, my God, why have you forsaken me?" (Matthew 27:46, NIV)

Had God really forsaken Jesus? Of course not. Yet Christ *felt* that God was distant because of the weight of the burden of shame and pain He took on. So when the Bible describes Jesus as a "man of sorrows, and acquainted with grief" (Isaiah 53:3, KJV), we can know that we are deeply loved by a God who understands how we feel. Feelings of grief and pain do not mean that God is far away; perhaps He is closer than He's ever been.

I'm learning not to be afraid of the silence. I choose, instead, to perceive it as intimate time with God. I like to think of Him being close and quiet, watching over me adoringly, the way I sneak in to watch my little daughter while she's sleeping.

So where *is* God when it hurts? I like the way Dr. Paul Brand explains it. He says that God is in *us* who are hurting, not in *it* that is hurting us.

I came to realize that the *real* questions are, *Where am I when it hurts? How am I responding?*

As a nurse educator I've taught many people that stress is not what happens *to* you, but rather your *response* to what happens. Our choices chart the direction our lives go.

The foundation of any 12-step recovery program is based on this personal power of choice: self-responsibility, accountability and—above all else—yielding control to the Higher Power. We are not victims blowing in the wind.

Frequently I make excuses or blame something or someone for the current state I'm in. And although many circumstances and experiences have influenced me, it's my responses and my choices that determine my state right now, as well as in the future.

I believe that we're confronted with very basic choices when we experience change or loss. I envision at least four possible ways to react.

We can choose to be a victim, becoming angry, bitter, and resentful. I've watched people hold onto their wounds,

and shrivel up like juiceless old prunes. They have no intention of feeling anything but miserable. Anger and confusion
are normal responses, but to get stuck there means we've
chosen to stop trusting and growing.

We can choose to believe that God is good, but not powerful enough, to change circumstances. Or we can believe
He's powerful enough, but not good enough to prevent
horrible things from happening to His people.

Third, we can choose to stay right where we are until we
understand God and all His workings. Now that could be a
long wait!

Or we can choose to trust God is who He says He is,
always operating out of love and wisdom, and that someday
all the misunderstandings and tragedies of this world will be
made plain to us.

Philip Yancey says, "Faith means believing in advance
what will only make sense in reverse."[1]

So many people exist frozen in time. It's as if their ability
to breathe and move has been placed in suspended anima-
tion, all because they *choose* to hold onto their pain, anger,
guilt, or regret.

While there's nothing I can do to reverse the loss of Trevor,
there *is* much I can do to keep *living*. What we do with the
unchangeable circumstances of our lives makes the difference between a life of despair or hope, bitterness or joy,
apathy or positive passion.

Because I felt the need to meet others who were in
similar pain, I went to a bereavement support group for
parents four weeks after Trevor's death. The image of what
I observed has stayed with me to this day.

A dozen or so couples participated. Each had lost a child—
some through accident, some illness. What struck me was
the different ways those parents reacted to their loss.

I recall two or three couples in particular who were 10
years or more removed from their child's death, but they

carried themselves as if it had happened yesterday! Their faces were haggard and worn; they spoke of the anger and confusion, as well as the bitterness. They were clinging to their pain, determined to forever feel broken and beaten.

Then there were others whose pain was more recent, and they showed signs that I could relate to—especially shock and numbness. They acted as if they had suddenly been transported to a foreign land, unable to speak the language, not knowing what to do next.

Still others had clearly grown more sensitive and settled about life as a result of their experience. They exhibited a strength that was evident before they even spoke. It was the look in their eyes that said to me, "You'll not always feel this way; life can still be worth living."

Meeting with that support group, I realized the thing we all dread most is change—yet change is the one thing in this life we can count on for sure! All these parents had changed, but the direction of their lives, and the quality of their lives, had everything to do with their choice of response.

Many of the books on suffering I've read in the past few years have included a discussion of the remarkable book *Man's Search for Meaning*, by Viktor Frankl. Frankl recounts his experiences in Nazi concentration camps. He speaks of the prisoners' realization that everything would be taken away, and of the literal nakedness that was their existence.

> ". . .most men in a concentration camp believed that the real opportunities in life had passed. Yet, in reality, there was an opportunity and a challenge. One could make a   victory of those experiences turning life into an inner triumph, or one could ignore the challenge and simply vegetate, as did the majority of prisoners."[2]

He spoke of the raw reality of *choice*—that our lives are not determined for us; we decide how we will live. The circumstances we find ourselves in are irrelevant. We *choose* what we will become in the next moment. He recalls the prisoners who chose to help others, comforting them, and giving away food from their own meager portions.

> *"They may have been few in number, but they offer sufficient proof that everything can be taken from a man but one thing: the last of the human freedoms—to choose one's attitude in any given set of circumstances, to choose one's own way."*[3]

I'm moved and inspired by the spirit of courage and determination of those few—to believe that the essence of their lives was not determined by their circumstances. They chose to believe that their suffering had meaning. They chose to be enlarged by the unfairness, not diminished by it.

But are you willing to make that choice yourself? The concept is illustrated by the story of the man who stretches a rope across Niagara Falls. He walks over to you, a bystander, and asks if you believe he can get across the falls pushing his wheelbarrow in front of him. Since you've seen him accomplish many seemingly impossible feats before, you answer, "Yes, I believe you can make it."

Then he asks if you'd be willing to show your trust by riding across in the wheelbarrow! And that's when the "rubber meets the road," when you must choose whether or not to trust.

I believe God is wanting each one of us to make a choice about his Lordship in our lives. Review His invitation:

> *"'For I know the plans I have for you,' declares the Lord, 'plans to prosper you and not to harm you, plans to give you hope and a future. Then you will [choose to] call upon me and [choose to] come and pray to me, and I will listen to you. You will [choose to] seek me and find me when you seek me with all your heart.'"*
> —*Jeremiah 29:11-13, NIV* [emphasis supplied]

I'm not the person I used to be before experiencing the death of Trevor. I'm learning to be thankful for that. The direction God wants to take me is towards His heart, and ultimately His home!

God's promises of the future—and hope for each day—are there to give me strength and purpose.

But they do not eliminate all pain.

Chapter Twelve

The Necessity of Suffering

"In all their affliction he was afflicted."
—Isaiah 63:9, KJV

**"Take thine own way with me, dear Lord,
Thou canst not otherwise than bless;
I launch me forth upon a sea
Of boundless love and tenderness."**
—Jean Sophia Pigot

Before I go on to discuss my favorite topic—our ultimate home—there's one other element of the issue of suffering that I feel the need to address. This is a difficult discussion that enters into a theology that would take volumes to traverse. But because of my own personal journey I feel compelled to mention the *necessity* of suffering.

We've discussed the idea of "the gift of pain" and how it becomes our teacher, revealing our condition. We've reflected on the hard questions—the why questions—and discovered those questions to be unanswerable in this life. We've seen how the direction of our lives, and our influence on others, is largely dependent on our expectations and responses. And we've determined that our responses, in large part, depend on our perception of God.

What we've not fully addressed are the high and holy purposes of suffering—the principle of "life out of death."

In other words, what relationship does suffering have to a more complete understanding of God's purposes for us?

Why would we resist the idea that our loving Heavenly Father would actually send or order a trial that would transform us more into His image, and make us more able to give comfort and hope to others? You see, whether He *sent* it or *allowed* it is irrelevant for me to know.

If I believe that this God who designed the universe, who keeps the stars on their courses and the seasons on their appointed schedule, truly *loves* me and wants nothing more than eternal relationship with me, why would I want Him to spare me anything that would fulfill His purpose in my life and in the world?

This question touches all the other topics we've discussed in this section. It points up the necessity of our complete surrender to His all-sufficiency. We must be settled on the ultimate question: "Will I let God be in control of my life, even if it means pain and disruption of my agenda? Can I accept that every event—no matter how large or small—has a purpose?" If I do not resist His teaching, He will draw me closer to His will for me.

Elisabeth Elliot is well acquainted with grief and loss. She's lost two husbands to death—one to the slaughtering spears of the Auca Indians in the remote jungles of South America, one after a long journey with cancer. She's written many books in which she speaks from her soul, making no attempt to dilute her convictions or her commitment to the all-sufficiency of Jesus, her Lord.

Elliot describes a necessary link between suffering and glory. She says that Christ came to bring another kind of life—His way of seeing this world. Jesus spoke of the blessedness of those who mourn, are poor and persecuted. He gave His disciples an illustration from the farmland around them: "I tell you the truth, unless a kernel of wheat falls to the ground and dies, it remains only a single seed. But if it dies, it produces many seeds." (John 12:24, NIV)

This deepest of mysteries brings us back to the cross over and over again. As we are called to follow Him in His life, we are also called to follow Him in His sufferings.

We know God's ways are not our ways. He orchestrates what may seem to be a roadblock—setback, persecution, or loss—to position us where we need to be to accomplish His purpose.

His ultimate purpose is always to reveal love and destroy the power of evil. Notice I did not say destroy evil. That day is coming. For now, however, the power of evil can be silenced in our lives as we surrender all we have and are to the One who loves us perfectly. We may not see His purposes immediately, or in a few years, or even in our lifetime—but all His dealings fit together like a harmonious song, declaring His kingdom.

I have a picture of a single rose on a long stem. Underneath are these words: "A life filled with love will have some thorns, but a life empty of love will have no roses." After looking at that picture many times and thinking about the saying, I no longer despise thorns!

As a singer, I now enjoy singing so much more because of an experience I had with laryngitis a few years ago. For eight long days I couldn't speak, and I was unable to sing for almost two months. Occasionally now when I'm singing I remember what it was like not to be able to do so, and my singing takes on deeper meaning. I pray that those who hear may be blessed in ways they would not otherwise. Ellen White writes about learning to sing in solitude:

> *"In the full light of day, and in hearing of the music of other voices, the caged bird will not sing the song that his master seeks to teach him. He learns a snatch of this, a trill of that, but never a separate and entire melody. But the master covers the cage, and places it*

where the bird will listen to the one song he is to sing. In the dark, he tries and tries again to sing that song until it is learned, and he breaks forth in   perfect melody. Then the bird is brought forth, and ever after he can sing that song in the light. Thus God deals with His children. He has a song to teach us, and when we have learned it amid the shadows of affliction, we can sing it ever afterward."[1]

Could it be that this experience we call suffering is what we need to mature? This is how God grows His children. This is how we get to the heart of what really matters and come to see what is true about God and ourselves. Maybe we should send condolence cards to those who have never suffered loss! There is so much of their souls and the heart of God that they have yet to discover.

Elliot concludes that suffering is necessary, that it is the key to really living:

". . .the best fruit will be what is produced by the best-pruned branch. The strongest steel be that which went through the hottest fire and the coldest water. The deepest knowledge of God's presence will have been acquired in the deepest river or dungeon or lion's den. The greatest joy will have come forth out of the greatest sorrow."[2]

I no longer view God as one who looks down and says, "Oh my, something difficult has happened to Sandy; I'd better get right down there and turn it into good."

I choose now to believe I'm not floating in the sea of life, a victim of random chance and chaos, who "just happens" to have a God who takes mercy on me and pulls me out.

The God I serve is sovereign over all the affairs of this world—including my life. Nothing touches me but that it has passed through Him first. (Whether He *causes* it to happen, or *allows* it to happen, is no longer important. I believe that both occur.)

What matters is that I accept that my life is in His hands. His purposes are being fulfilled in every aspect of my life, whether or not I understand. Those purposes concern the soul, and matters of the soul are accessed most effectively in the stormy seasons of our lives.

Deeper yet is the mystery of the glory in the sharing of Christ's sufferings. Somehow in God's kingdom death creates life.

We see this demonstrated regularly in nature—the seed must crack to send forth the shoot, the leaf bud must break to let go the leaf, the petals drop off the flower to let the fruit form.

And so it must be in our lives. When we die to ourselves we are alive to serve God and others. This awesome Kingdom that God wants to establish in our hearts is secured through fire and storm, through sorrow and heartache. Only then, if we do not resist His grace, will we be unshakable. Only then will we possess the strength and comfort to give to others. Only then will we experience real joy.

And only then will we be able to sing throughout eternity the song that even the angels cannot sing! With glorious orchestration—and no doubt 10-part harmony—we will lift our voices to proclaim that our eternal life was secured through the death and resurrection of our Lord; that we have been privileged to experience a small part of His suffering; and that He has brought us through!

> *"Therefore God exalted him to the highest place and gave him the name that is above every name, that at the name of Jesus every knee should bow, in heaven and on earth and under the earth, and every tongue confess that Jesus Christ is Lord, to the glory of God the Father."*
> *—Philippians 2:9-11, NIV*

This passage and others from the Bible give me great comfort and something tangible to look forward to. A great day is coming—Heaven has the final word!

Chapter Thirteen

The Final Word

**"And faith is, in the end, a kind of homesickness—
for a home we have never visited, but have
never once stopped longing for."**
—Philip Yancey

". . .and God shall wipe away all tears from their eyes."
—Revelation 7:17, KJV

As a little girl I memorized this Bible verse:

> *"Do not let not your hearts be troubled. Trust in God;
> trust also in me. In my Father's house are many rooms;
> if it were not so, I would have told you. I am going
> there to prepare a place for you. And if I go and pre-
> pare a place for you, I will come back and take you to
> be with me that you also may be where I am."*
> —*John 14:1-3 NIV*

Like many verses I memorized, it had a nice rhythm and
ring to it, and it spoke of something very nice; but as a child,
I didn't yet have a longing for such a place. Life here was
warm and safe and loving.

Then as a pre-teen, I remember building a word picture
for an assignment in Bible class:

H *Hallelujah! We'll finally be home!*
E *Every knee will bow*
A *Always in the presence of God*
V *Victory over sin and suffering forever*
E *Every tongue will confess that Jesus is Lord*
N *Never to part again!*

As an adult, I realize that if I choose to believe anything at all in the Bible as true, then it is *all* true. And that means that heaven is a real place! My heart beats faster as I contemplate the reality of it.

In any Christian discussion of suffering, heaven is the last word. In the midst of his agony, Job knew that someday he would see God face to face.

> *"For I know that my Redeemer liveth, and that he shall stand at the latter day upon the earth: and though after my skin worms destroy this body, yet in my flesh shall I see God: whom I shall see for myself, and mine eyes shall behold, and not another; though my reins be consumed within me."*
> —*Job 19:25-27, KJV*

How does one think realistically about heaven? It has been promised, yet none of us has been there and returned to tell about it. It seems so far away, and so unreal most of the time.

I frequently sing the words of a song that says, "I'm but a stranger here; heaven is my home." Sometimes I wonder how much of a stranger I really feel here? Last year I had an opportunity to find out.

I was invited to go to Russia for two weeks with a small group of professionals to help set up a diabetes program at an eight hundred bed hospital outside Moscow. I could spend the next ten pages describing the situations we encountered.

Nothing was familiar, except for the buildings, which could have been located in many parts of this country.

Homelike touches and comforts were lacking; the food was different, methods of transportation were different, the customs were different, the music was different, the decorations and items for gifts were different. Certainly the atmosphere and conditions of the hospital were vastly different from what is familiar to us.

The people we met were warm and kind and appreciative, but there was no light in their eyes. One lady said, "We've stopped dreaming."

There wasn't an hour of the day that I didn't wonder how things were back home. Why? Because home was where my heart was—with my children and evidence of my hopes and dreams.

We were able to enjoy and learn from the trip because we knew we were going home soon. Home, where everyday living for us was beyond the imagination of those people.

After returning from Russia I have less trouble imagining a land that is beyond *my* imagination. Scripture says:

> *"No eye has seen, no ear has heard, no mind has conceived what God has prepared for those who love him. . ."*
> —*I Corinthians 2:9 NIV*

Exciting research is being done in the area of imaging. Patients with infectious or terminal illnesses are being taught to image their white blood cells fighting the sick cells. As a result their blood chemistry has improved! People who've undergone physical and mental torture have survived by keeping their minds focused on their hopes and dreams—and envisioning their survival.

It seems strange, then, that we Christians spend so little time envisioning heaven, our *real* home. Someday our stay here will seem like a wink of time compared to all of eternity. But this is the learning ground. This is where the choices are made that will prepare us for that "better land."

Heaven—the word itself conjures up different images for each person. In preparing for this chapter I asked people who believed in heaven as a literal place what they thought about when I said "heaven." Here are some of the responses:

- No more sickness or death
- I'll always feel rested
- Perfect, healthy bodies
- Unbelievable beauty everywhere
- Fabulous food!
- Incredible music
- I can play with the animals that are now wild
- Reunion with loved ones
- Meeting all the people from the Bible
- Study the science of things not known to us now
- Meeting my guardian angel
- Spending time with Jesus

Everyone has a different idea of what heaven will be like and what we will be doing there, based on his or her life experiences. Some of the answers reflected anticipated relief, such as the absence of pain and suffering. Oh, how we long for that time, when there will be no more tears!

Another text I memorized as a child, but now more fully understand, says:

"Do not store up for yourselves treasures on earth, where moth and rust destroy, and where thieves break in and steal. But store up for yourselves treasures in heaven. . .For where your treasure is, there your heart will be also."
—Matthew 6:19-21, NIV

Wherever our time, passion, energy, and dreams are spent, that is where we're striving. Henry Ward Beecher said, "Heaven will be inherited by every person who has heaven in his soul." I believe that we won't be happy in heaven —living in the presence of eternal grace and love—if we haven't allowed the Kingdom of God to begin in our hearts here on earth.

> *"My sheep listen to my voice; I know them, and they follow me. I give them eternal life, and they shall never perish; no one can snatch them out of my hand. My Father, who has given them to me, is greater than all; no one can snatch them out of my Father's hand."*
> *—John 10:27-29, NIV*

I never understood the phrase "homesick for heaven" until the loss of Trevor. He and I used to talk about heaven, especially those last two weeks of his life. It helped to make it more real to us to envision it. We talked about what we would do there, tried to imagine how it would look, sound and smell. We named all the wild animals we couldn't wait to play with. I told him there would be many people who'd been inspired by his faith and courage waiting to greet him.

There's a song that says, "This world is not my home, I'm just a passing through, My treasures are laid up somewhere beyond the blue. . ." Too often we forget that this life is not permanent.

Despite our temporary status here, the separation from our loved ones who have died is a bitter experience. We have a gnawing hunger to hold them again. I'm comforted to know that God does not view death as we do. To us it is the ultimate enemy. But the *real* threat is to live a life separated from God—to resist Him once and for all, and to choose to miss out on an eternity with Him.

I like what Philip Yancey says: "We need more than a

miracle. We need a new heaven and a new earth, and until we have those, unfairness will not disappear."[1]

H.M.S. Richards, Sr., founding speaker for the Voice of Prophecy radio broadcast, was nearing the end of his long life. One visitor said to him, "Oh, Pastor Richards, you've been preaching about the second coming of Christ for all these years, and now you won't get to see Him come."

Pastor Richards answered, "Oh, yes I will! I'm just going to take a little nap!"

And that's all it is to those who fall asleep near to the heart of God. Just a little nap. No passing of time for them. Trevor said the next thing he would hear would be God's voice saying "Wake up, Trevie, it's time to go home!"

In 1992 Tim Crosby from the Voice of Prophecy sent me a song he'd just written entitled "Some Holy Morning." He thought it would fit my voice and hoped I'd want to sing it. I was moved by the song, but for some reason shelved it.

In June 1993 Trevor died his courageous death, and his experience of faith was an inspiration to all who knew him. Four months later I was asked to participate in an interview with Lonnie Melashenko at the Voice of Prophecy. Pastor Melashenko wanted me to tell Trevor's story. As we were discussing the taping he said, "Why don't you sing that song Tim wrote?"

I hadn't listened to it since shelving it the year before. Now I know what it was being saved for. It has become the song of the deepest places of my heart.

> Some holy morning
> I'm gonna fly far away;
> Some blessed morning,
> To a never, never, never-ending day.
>
> Some great-day morning
> He's gonna call on my name;

Some lovely morning,
I'll never, never, never be the same.

Gon' meet my Saviour in glory;
Gon' see Him break through the blue;
And I'll help tell the story
Of how He died for me and you.

Some golden morning
I'll meet the hope of my heart;
Some blissful morning,
We never, never, nevermore will part.

Gon' be no more tears and sorrow,
Gon' lay my old burdens down;
And I'll always have tomorrow
To play my harp, and wear my crown.

Some holy morning
I'm gonna fly far away;
Some blessed morning,
To a never, never, never-ending day.*

What a reunion awaits us! To gather with those of all ages who trusted God. I'm going to talk *with* Job instead of reading about him! Trevor and I will take up right where we left off—holding one another and clinging to the hope we had that will be a glorious reality.

> *"Never again will they hunger; never again will they thirst. The sun will not beat upon them, nor any scorching heat. For the Lamb at the center of the throne will be their shepherd; he will lead them to springs of living water. And God will wipe away every tear from their eyes."*
> —*Revelation 7:16-17, NIV*

*Copyright 1994 by Tim Crosby. Used by permission.

As I contemplate that wonderful, tearless place, I feel I've come to the end of my struggle to find meaning in Trevor's life and death. I believe the larger answer to our prayer for physical healing for Trevor was not "No," but rather "Not yet." When I think of all I can't see Trevor do, God reminds me, "Oh, yes, you will—and in such a better place!"

John the Revelator describes that place with words that raise bumps on my arms when I read them:

> "Then I saw a new heaven and a new earth,…I saw the Holy City, the new Jerusalem, coming down out of heaven from God, prepared as a bride beautifully dressed for her husband. And I heard a loud voice from the throne saying, 'Now the dwelling of God is with men, and he will live with them. They will be his people, and God himself will be with them and be their God. He will wipe every tear from their eyes. There will be no more death or mourning or crying or pain, for the old order of things has passed away.'"
> —Revelation 21:1-4, *NIV*

Trevor said, "If only one person finds God as a result of my experience, then it will be worth it!" I can assure you that I am that one person, a very different mom from the one Trevor knew.

But I also know there will be many more who will be looking for Trevor, who said he wanted to be a greeter at the gates of heaven. I want to make a date with you to meet him there.

He'll be looking for you!

Heal Me
I Need to Grow

Section Three

Come, ye disconsolate,
where'er ye languish;
Come to the mercy seat,
fervently kneel;
Here bring your wounded hearts,
here tell your anguish;
Earth has no sorrow that
heaven cannot heal.

Joy of the comfortless,
light of the straying,
Hope of the penitent,
fadeless and pure!
Here speaks the Comforter,
tenderly saying,
"Earth has no sorrow that
heaven cannot cure."

Here see the Bread of Life;
see waters flowing
Forth from the throne of God,
pure from above;
Come to the feast of love—
come, ever knowing
Earth has no sorrow but
heaven can remove.

Chapter Fourteen

Preparing for Loss

"Who hath God hath all; who hath Him not, hath less than nothing."
—Ancient Proverb

"Oh the sheer joy of it! Living with Thee, God of the universe, Lord of a tree. Maker of mountains, Lover of me"
—Ralph Cushman

Experiencing significant loss is inevitable—it *will* come. But think about this analogy: Although we can't prevent a downpour, we can position ourselves under an umbrella so that when the rain comes, we may get damp, but we won't be drenched.

John Killinger in his book *For God's Sake—Be Human* shares some thoughts about how we handle life's adversities. He describes the irony of how joy is born out of sorrow and toil as much as it is out of pleasure and ease. He's quick to say, however, that passing through deep waters doesn't mean you'll magically have fullness of life. But he reminds us that our great God is present in *all* of life—even the tragedies—and it is His presence that transforms such storms into opportunities for worship.

How we've worshipped God in times of peace will largely determine how we'll respond in times of challenge and crisis. In earlier chapters we've seen the different ways people respond to adversity. The same horrific event can deepen and strengthen one person, while another becomes bitter, resentful and unable to experience further joy.

Richard Exley expands this thought:

"What makes the difference? Resources. Inner resources developed across a lifetime through spiritual disciplines. If you haven't worshipped regularly in the sunshine of your life, you probably won't be able to worship in the darkness."[1]

What is meant by "worship"? Is it regular attendance at church? Church is one place to worship God. But have you noticed how some people make church attendance their whole worship experience? True worship is an attitude, a posture of continual surrender and praise.

I found this to be true for me in the hour of my greatest need, during the illness and death of Trevor. I had four generations of faithful Christians to claim as my lineage. I'd been raised with living examples all around me of this attitude of worship. There'd been mountaintop experiences in my own spiritual life, as well as dry spells—times when I was depending on my own strength and neglecting a day-by-day surrender to God.

At the time of crisis I was in a dry spot. I could quote Bible chapter and verse, but I hadn't been dancing with the Lord in a while. Most of what I was doing spiritually was sheer habit. I believed it, but it wasn't *alive.*

In the darkest hour, I felt myself scrambling more than I would have needed to in order to connect with God on a heart-to-heart level. Yet by His grace He accepted my feeble, faltering choice to let Him lead. I experienced the truth of this verse, ". . .my strength is made perfect in weakness." (2 Corinthians 12:9, *KJV*)

Crisis reveals where you are with God—and your life. You're more likely to trust God to navigate for you and keep you afloat during the big storms if you've been trusting Him during the calms.

In his book *Recovering From the Losses of Life,* noted Christian counselor and author, Norman Wright, lists 11 characteristics of survivors. As I reflect on the last four years of my life, the six outlined below have made the most difference in my healing. These characteristics need to be in development during the less significant losses we experience day to day.

Survivors are prepared. They plan ahead for the possibility of unpredictable events—and they also have a plan of how to proceed through the predictable transitions of life. For example, they have financial plans that provide for education, retirement and the loss of a spouse.

Survivors learn from the experience and wisdom of others. They pay attention and notice what others are going through and learn from those observations.

Survivors have a desire to learn and grow. They develop an attitude that keeps them willing to see something in different ways. When loss comes, *everything* has to be examined from a new perspective.

Survivors do not seek to blame. Blaming would only keep them stuck in their grief, not moving through and beyond it.

Survivors choose to go on. They possess the determination to survive and find some way to excel or express themselves.

True survivors have a personal faith in God. They continue to trust Him regardless of the circumstances.

While all these characteristics are good to cultivate ahead of time, there are also practical, day-to-day things that can help you prepare for loss. I've compiled a list of practical suggestions that work for me. I've collected some of them from my reading and experiences shared by others, but most of these I've discovered on my own journey, especially as I look back and reflect on what would have better prepared me. I hope they'll be helpful to you.

PRACTICAL WAYS TO BE PREPARED:

Spend a few minutes regularly contemplating how you'll respond to loss and change. Envision yourself in the midst of crisis and feel your response. Base your response on how you hope to respond. Discuss this with your spouse, your children and/or someone else close to you. Your reflection should bring you to an affirmation of who you really are.

- Who will you be if you're no longer a mother?
- Who will you be when you're no longer a practicing physician?
- Who will you be if you can no longer run or walk?

How do you define yourself? Do you define yourself by your spouse, your children, your work, your talents, appearance, performance, or income?

If you build your identity and value on anything or anyone that is changeable, you'll be floating in the sea of life—without a clear identity—if that thing or person is lost. Our real identity, now and forever, is simply to be a child of our Heavenly Father, and *nothing* can change that or lessen His passion for us!

Each day tell one person one thing you appreciate about him/her. For example, I now concentrate on my two children. Today I said to Taryn, "Thank you for the way you tell me you love me, all by yourself. That makes Mommy feel good."

Build trusting and supportive relationships with people with whom you can be real, honest, and vulnerable, who accept you without judgment. To build this kind of relationship takes time and energy, but it offers rich rewards.

Spend plenty of time with those dearest to you. Take lots of pictures. Create scrapbooks or albums of pictures and memories of trips and other special times together. Write down your spouse's and children's unique sayings and characteristics.

Share who you really are with those you love. Show your real feelings. Not doing so is one of the most common regrets that people have. Have heart-to-heart talks about mutual interests, joys, sorrows and fears.

Say the things to them that you imagine you would regret not having said if they should die. As Larry Yeagley says in his handbook for those who grieve, "This openness about every aspect of life will eliminate the game playing and 'conspiracy of silence' that occurs during crisis in far too many families."[2]

Learn independence. While fostering a trusting and supportive relationship with your spouse, it's critical also to learn independence. How many spouses have been left devastated and unprepared to carry on normal daily responsibilities because of depending completely on the other person? Today's women are encouraged to become more involved in family finances and investments, and men are learning housekeeping and child-rearing skills. Sharing all aspects of life will make you a stronger person, even if you and your spouse grow old together. And if you end up alone, you'll be better equipped to live independently.

Fortify yourself with the promises of God. Read the "comfort texts" found at the end of this book. They'll act as preventative medicine for future wounds. Plan to memorize one each week and repeat it to yourself during the day.

Develop a thankful spirit. Find two things each day to be thankful for. Write them down. At first your list may be one that almost anybody could write—"Today I'm thankful for sunshine and bird song"—but you'll develop the knack of seeing the uniqueness of your own life. Soon you'll be writing things such as "I'm thankful that I have the time today to visit a sick friend" and "Thanks for the thunderstorm that left a rainbow painted across our valley."

Develop your own strategy for visiting people who are in hard times. Spend time with patients in the hospital, homeless in shelters and those confined to their homes. Experiencing the sorrows of others will enlarge your view of the world and, when you get involved with others in need, your response to your own hard time won't be as full of self-pity. Many parents who've lost a child have experienced healing by reaching out to others surviving a similar loss.

Deal effectively with smaller losses in your life.
Life is full of things and relationships that break apart—
your grandmother's Wedgwood teacup that shattered
in the sink, the promotion you *didn't* get, your forced
immobility from a broken leg, the strained relationship with your sister, the love interest who isn't
returning your glances. How you respond to these
disappointments sets up a pattern for how you'll
respond to all the losses in your life. Make sure you're
not holding onto unresolved grief over a small or
medium-sized loss.

Develop your inner person. Create interests that are
uniquely yours, so that *you* will remain even if someone close to you is lost. Music, books, journalizing,
painting—explore yourself through these avenues now.
These creative outlets will be a familiar and comfortable haven to nurture you in time of grief. Do something creative you've always wanted to do but kept
putting off.

Learn to stay in the moment. We're so programmed
to look for the fantastic—the "can-you-top-this?" experiences—that we miss out on the sacredness of everyday moments. To be fully in the present moment takes
some practice.

Since I've become more aware of this concept, I've
noticed that I'm often thinking of something else. I'm
thinking ahead—or I'm thinking back—but not con-
sciously thinking about the very moment I'm in and
really experiencing it. So, I've started to say, "*In this
moment*, I'm feeling the warm sun on my face and
hearing the birds sing." "*In this moment*, I'm here shoot-
ing baskets with my son." (Ask him who's winning!)

What a difference this has made in my life. Life is captured and embraced—and is so much more satisfying! I seem to be less concerned with how *many* moments there will be because each one is more meaningful.

This is the practice of "mindfulness" which has become a buzzword in the self-help literature of the 90s. Since God has grace and strength for this moment only, it makes sense that we would want to be totally awake and aware of our need in the present moment.

Try this practice and you'll find that the ordinary becomes the extraordinary, and all of life takes on a sacredness. Watching a flock of birds flying into the sunset becomes a holy moment. The single flower pushing its way up through the crack in your driveway is cause enough to pause and wonder. The small, scribbly drawing that your two-year old brings you becomes a cherished classic.

Then, when life hands you difficult, disturbing moments, you'll have practiced being comfortable in the present, and you'll not run. Rather you'll be able to embrace and experience fully what God desires to give you. You'll recognize it as a gift—with a holy purpose—because you've developed a way of seeing meaning in *all* of life's moments.

On a very personal note, take care of your physical body now. The more physically fit you are, the better equipped you'll be to endure severe stress.

- Exercise regularly
- Eat a healthful diet
- Get enough sleep
- Drink plenty of water
- Learn to relax

When practiced regularly, relaxation techniques can lower your blood pressure and your heart rate. Although there are many relaxation exercises, this is one I use frequently with my patients:

1. Lie down or sit in a quiet, comfortable place where you can relax. Allow no interruptions for ten minutes. Take the phone off the hook! Turn on relaxing music if this is soothing to you.

2. Close your eyes and imagine a peaceful place you'd like to be. This may be in a meadow, beside a babbling brook, in the mountains surrounded by immense pines, or at the ocean with the rhythmic pulse of the waves. Hear the sounds of your special place. Smell the smells.

3. Imagine an empty box next to you. Take all of your worries and stressors and just for now put them in the box and close the lid. You can get them out later, when you want to.

4. Now take three deep, full breaths. (You may need to put your hands on your abdomen to make sure you're breathing correctly. Your abdomen should expand when you take a breath in.) Count to 6 as you breathe in, hold the breath for 6 counts, and take 6 counts to exhale slowly. This helps you to focus and trains your abdominal muscles.

It's a good idea during the day to practice about ten of these deep breaths at a time; gradually you'll be able to increase your number.

Be very conscious of the sound of your breathing, and think of all the tension leaving your body as you exhale.

5. Now, starting with your feet and working your way up your body, isolate various muscle groups, tensing them tightly for a few seconds and then releasing them. First your toes and feet; then your calves and thighs; next your buttocks; then your abdomen; then your shoulders; next your neck; then your face; and finally your hands and arms. After each muscle group, take a deep cleansing breath. End your session with three more deep breaths. By now you should feel relaxed and calm.

If the journey of grief should be yours to travel, your trip will be more successful if you've "packed ahead" in these ways; they'll be effective habits that will serve you well.

If you're in that valley of grief now, follow me into the next chapter and learn how to give yourself the help that is healing.

Chapter Fifteen

Helping Yourself in Loss

"If you want to see stars, darkness is required."
—Author unknown

**"He that goeth forth and weepeth,
bearing precious seed,
shall doubtless come again with rejoicing,
bringing his sheaves with him."**
—Psalm 126:6, KJV

About a year after Trevor's death I was feeling meltdown. The stark reality had set in that he really *was* gone—and he *wasn't* coming back. I'd been through the well-documented stages of grief—shock, denial, anger/depression, bargaining, and acceptance. I found that these were not static stages, but rather a cycle that I passed through again and again, although the intensity of the cycles had softened slightly.

As time went by, it seemed as if the grief deepened. That's a troubling place to be: where you feel you can't live *with* the memories, but you can't live *without* them either. I was agitated and restless—not able to control or quiet these moods. It was as if the very chemistry of my body remembered and was groaning. I felt a brooding anxiety, a phantom-like pain. I've heard amputees describe this phantom-like pain in the location where a leg—now gone—used to be.

That first year I couldn't bring myself to take pictures of Todd and Taryn. With Trevor missing, it just wasn't a complete picture. I hadn't accepted my reality as it now was. At some point in time reality must be recognized and the limits lived. The picture *is* complete with the present reality of two children.

Depression rarely follows loss immediately. It comes at the end of the struggle, after the denial yields to reality and the bargaining doesn't pay off and the escapes all lead to nowhere. Then there is no more strength to fight off the inevitable and undeniable.

I realized that I could be heading for clinical depression. I sought professional help and focused my energies on my own healing, which was difficult for me to do.

I found myself needing to denounce everything trivial in the world—and embracing all that is vital. A few months after Trevor died, I was sitting behind a couple with two small children. The little boy couldn't decide where to sit, and he was up and down, up and down, till finally his father exploded, grabbed him by the arm, swore at him, and sat him down hard! I wanted so badly to yell, "I lost my 7-year-old to brain cancer recently, and believe me, it doesn't matter where your son sits!"

I wanted others to know what a defining moment had occurred in my life, but I soon realized that my declarations would serve mostly to affirm my own experience. Others would hear me, but each one would have to experience his or her own defining moment in order to be changed.

As time has gone by, the mundane experiences in life that at first had little meaning are now becoming sacred. Nothing seems trivial. Tucking Taryn into bed and helping Todd with math I don't understand—these have become precious, profound moments. This kind of awe of life is not uncommon to those experiencing loss.

To better understand what happens following a loss, let's

look at this process we call grief. And Scripture is a good place to start.

The Bible contains many examples of real people who openly showed their grief. King David mourned for his son Amnon every day (2 Samuel 13: 29-39). He even grieved deeply over the death of his rebellious son Absalom, who tried to overthrow his father's throne. The king went to his chamber and wept: "O my son Absalom, my son, my son Absalom! would God I had died for thee, O Absalom, my son, my son!" (2 Samuel 18:33, *KJV*)

Jesus wept at hearing of the death of his friend Lazarus (John 11:30-38). Mary Magdalene wept as she came close to the tomb of Jesus, her Lord. (John 20:11-16).

Grieving is a *process*, a necessary journey. There is no fixed schedule, and there is no right or wrong way to grieve. There will be as many different reactions and ways to grieve as there are people who mourn. However, most people initially experience some—or all—of these recognized reactions: shock, disbelief, denial, numbnesss, anger, depression, and guilt. The true purpose of grieving is to get beyond—not *over*—these normal reactions, to face the loss, and to make the necessary adaptations so the loss can be lived with in a healthy way.

It's also common to acutely experience these symptoms: sleeplessness, loss of appetite, extreme fatigue, memory loss, mood changes and reduced productivity. As I mentioned in the last chapter, if the smaller losses of life have not been grieved and resolved, each future loss will reactivate the unresolved issues, which make the present loss even harder to bear.

For comprehensive coverage on the clinical aspects of grieving, I highly recommend the book *Recovering from the Losses of Life*. Norman Wright addresses in depth the symptoms of unresolved grief. In essence, these are behaviors or attitudes that are stuck. We can become stuck in denial, anger, or depression. Through my own experience, I have come to believe that it takes more energy to hang on to your pain than it does to lean into it—and let it go.

There are some specific steps to use grief to grow us into stronger people. Here are some of the most necessary:

First, it is necessary to change the relationship with the person that was lost. Just as you had a certain way of living with the person before the loss, you now have to make a way or pattern of living *without* that loved one.

Second, incorporate the loss into your very being and develop a sense of self that reflects the changes you've made. It will be a new definition of *you.* It's critical that you become a different person, and yet you must never forget your loved one and the special relationship you shared. Some people are terrified that if they change they will ignore or forget the person they've lost. Because of that terror they try *not* to change. The results are not healthy.

Finally, find new ways to invest the emotional energies you once had with the one who was lost. Since I can no longer have the same relationship with Trevor that we once had, I've wanted to find ways to keep him alive in my memory in healthy ways. In order to do that, I had to accept fully he was gone—and would *not* be coming back. Then I thought about what parts of our life together I could still maintain.

One thing that has worked well for me is to return to the park where Trevor and I used to go. I sit and reflect—not to feel sorry for myself or to feel wounded but to find pleasure in the memories of Trevor learning to play soccer in that park. The memories of those good times bring a smile to my face.

I've also kept several tubs full of things he made—and crafts we did together—as well as a few articles of clothing that were his favorites. I haven't made a "shrine" with his things, but when I see his favorite shirt, it makes me glad that he was my son and I got to enjoy him for seven years.

Another way to experience a relationship with your memories is to get involved in activities that the one you lost enjoyed. Sometimes I sit and color for an hour or so, the way Trevor used to do. I've even taken a brief look at wrestling on TV, which I personally detest, but which Trevor loved to watch with his dad. To him, TV wrestling was like an adult cartoon, and when I see it now, I laugh and remember Trevor's face when he watched it.

I find myself fixing and eating some of his favorite foods. I don't do any of these things very often, but they are healthy ways of creating a new relationship with the love you will always have for that person.

I've found that in my own journey of grief there are some clear signs that recovery is taking place. You may not experience exactly the same reactions, but see whether you share any of these:

I can think of Trevor without agonizing pain, only sweet sadness. On occasions, the feelings of grief result in a huge wave of sadness as I review the closing events of his life. But these occasions are becoming less frequent as time goes by.

I feel energy returning—to invest in my present reality. For me it was about two years before I felt like I was emotionally incorporating the chronic ache into my life, and that I had renewed energy with which to tackle each day. In the best literature on grieving, the two-year mark is commonly referred to as the time when the fresh air begins to blow back into your life.

My thinking is clearing; I don't feel as foggy-headed. Grieving is a physiological process. It requires great mental and emotional energy. In the early stages there just isn't enough energy left over to be as sharp and productive as you were before the loss.

I know I can once again trust my judgment. Especially in the first year I had a difficult time making important decisions, and I tended to be unsure of even the simpler ones. Experiencing a great loss is *unsettling*, and everything in your life shifts, like surviving a 9.5 earthquake and trying to settle your life again afterwards.

I look for ways to do for others, as well as to be with others. After a major loss, it takes time to have the strength and desire to give sustained attention to someone else.

I feel alive again and think in positive ways. Grieving has a life of its own. Even when it's ventured upon in a healthy way, there is no set timetable. Only you will know when you're beginning to take deeper breaths and your tendency to protect yourself is giving way to making yourself vulnerable again.

I find myself being grateful and thankful. Grieving begins to give way to gratitude—gratitude for having had Trevor in my life, gratitude for the incredible love and support from others, gratitude for the precious lives of Todd and Taryn, as well as gratitude for the way God is leading me today.

It usually takes two to three years for the general steps of grief work to take place—for the wounds to no longer be "gaping open," and the signs of recovery to be evident to you and others around you who have shared the loss.

My heart goes out to you as you journey through this profound experience. Practicing the following steps has been critical to my recovery. They represent those things that were the most helpful to me, and many of them are supported in the literature I've read on grieving. I pray that they will also benefit you:

PRACTICAL WAYS TO HELP YOURSELF

Early in the grief process:

At the time of death from illness, create a family atmosphere as much as possible. We had Trevor's favorite things from home in his hospital room. I brought family picture albums so others could look through them as they were there with him. We played praise music in the background.

If it's an option to take your loved one home to die, consider it carefully. Throughout the United States hospices are making significant differences in how a family can experience the dying process together. Hospice staff and volunteers provide physical, mental and spiritual support for the terminally ill person, as well as the family. A hospice team can help make dying a family event instead of a solitary process.

Lean into it. . .Be with your pain. . .Embrace it. Pain is part of your loving the one you lost. Avoid obvious escapes such as excessive TV, food, alcohol, and increased hours of work or business.

Resume usual family routines as soon as possible. There is comfort and safety in predictability and established routine. It's tempting to let everything become random and chaotic when you're in pain, but chaos will only exaggerate the discomfort.

Eliminate the unnecessary. Keep decision making to a minimum. Don't plunge into a frenzy of cleaning, organizing, or starting new projects.

Get as much rest as possible. Take some time off from work. Schedule rest into your day. You can't sleep or rest too much during this time. It's okay to be in slow motion for several weeks or months.

Don't try to do what you think *others* expect of you. Instead, listen to your own body and spirit. Go easy on yourself; be your own best friend.

Avoid stress-inducing foods. Some foods can increase your anxiety directly, or indirectly, by making you too sluggish to respond effectively.

Foods that are high in fat—such as French fries, chips, and other deep-fried food—are hard to digest, and can make you feel tired.

Also avoid alcohol and caffeine, which affect your nervous system.

Instead eat lots of citrus fruits, healthy choices of protein, and plenty of vegetables. Complex carbohydrates can help settle your nerves. Go for whole-grain breads and cereals, pasta, potatoes, yogurt, or even air-popped popcorn.

Take a multivitamin high in C, calcium, magnesium, and B complex. All of these aid the body in its stress response.

Drink lots of water, at least eight glasses a day. Your coping responses are diminished if you're not well hydrated.

To let yourself *heal*, you must let yourself *feel*. It's okay to feel *anything.* You may feel grief-stricken, angry, exhausted, muddled, lost, beaten, indecisive, relieved, overwhelmed, inferior, melancholy, silly. Or you may feel *nothing.* Give your feelings—whatever they are—all to God. It's okay to *feel* your fears, but to the degree you can, don't believe them.

Let others do for you. For some of us, it's easier to give than to receive, but especially at a time of loss others need the blessing of giving. Accept offers that will relieve you of burdens—and provide your friends the blessing of serving you.

If you can identify what you need, ask for specific help or support. Seek out the support and help of others. They can't read your mind, and they, too, may be feeling sad and uncomfortable not knowing what to do or say.

Don't forget to feed your soul. For you it may be through music, reading, painting, journaling, or walking out in nature.

Don't be ashamed about pampering yourself! Get a massage, take time alone, buy yourself a small luxury, go out to eat, visit an art museum, treat yourself to flowers, or indulge in a favorite snack or dessert. The ladies may want to add a hot bubble bath, or go and have their nails and hair done,

Begin to journal your journey through grief. Later it will be a comfort and strength to you to go back and see how you've evolved through this experience. It's amazing how you can more clearly see the hand of God in your life when you do this.

Spend time in the fresh air and sunshine. Take a walk or hike, ride your bike, or sit quietly by the ocean or a lake. You may not have the energy yet for long trips, but a couple of hours outside can do wonders for your spirit.

Let go of expectations of how you think people should be responding to you. Don't feel slighted about people who lack the courage to contact you. This is no time to be carrying—or building—grudges.

Seek guidance from one you respect. Find a trusted friend or relative who will encourage you. Open your heart to this carefully chosen confidant rather than depending upon the plethora of "helpful" advice from acquaintances. Beware of well-meaning statements that begin with: *should, you'd better,* or *it's time you. . .*Let such comments fly away with the wind.

Spend quiet time each day in prayer and meditation. Getting quiet may evoke tears, but that's good— it's cleansing. Spend more time listening than talking to God. He *will* speak to you.

Find one thing you are thankful for, and repeat it

out loud to yourself during the day. At first this will seem impossible, but you'll gradually realize that even in the midst of sorrow you are also surrounded by things you seldom notice or appreciate.

Thank God for His mercies and His unfolding plan in your life, even if you don't feel joyful and cannot see the plan. After Trevor died, it was many mornings and nights before I could thank God for anything— or even talk to Him about much of anything—but as I began to count my blessings, my burdens began to lift.

Don't diminish your loss. Avoid such phrases as *that's life, oh well, who cares?* or *it doesn't matter.*

Heal at your own pace. Try to be patient with impatient friends who want you to "get back to normal."

Cry. Crying releases tension and induces relaxation. Sometimes I'm taken off guard at the most unexpected moment—and tears come. It's important not to fight them back and postpone the feelings. You can't really postpone feelings. You just end up covering them over, but they are there just the same, and will affect your ability to function.

Sometimes I schedule a grieving session. I can feel the tension mounting, maybe during the week. I notice I'm out of focus. Usually it's because I haven't taken time out to experience my feelings. So I have a special place in the house I go. I turn on the music, get out pictures of Trevor and the family, and let it flow. I ask God to draw near to me and hold me during that time, revealing what He desires for me.

Sometimes I cry nonstop for an hour—it comes all the way up from my toes—but I usually end with smiles and thankfulness for things I hadn't even thought of before.

Go ahead and *laugh*! The line between tragedy and comedy is a thin one, and laughter is one of the best medicines around. Do whatever it takes to make you laugh. You're not being disloyal to the one you loved by laughing.

Surround yourself with things that are alive. Choose a bird, a cat or dog, plants or flowers, a goldfish. This is particularly important for a grieving person who lives alone, with less contact with other people. Your local animal shelter probably has a number of dogs and cats, and at a time of great stress it might be better to consider adopting a mature animal rather than that adorable kitten or puppy who needs lots of attention and training. If you don't want to adopt an animal, volunteer at the shelter to walk dogs or cuddle cats, perhaps one day a week.

If you need professional help, seek out a good counselor. You might need a professional if you're experiencing any of the following:

- If you fear harming yourself or others or frequently have suicidal thoughts.
- If you don't feel good about yourself or seem constantly out of control or stressed out.
- If you repeatedly find yourself in loss situations.
- If you seek comfort in alcohol, drugs, overeating or other potentially harmful activities.
- If the support of wise friends and family is not enough.

Communicate your feelings to your support community. Sometimes you wish you could tell people what you're experiencing and that they don't need to "fix" you. It might be helpful for you to write a letter expressing what you're experiencing. You may decide to keep the letter. But you might go ahead and send it to family and friends. Here's a sample letter. Feel free to use it if it works for you:

Dear Friends and Loved Ones,

I've recently suffered the devastating loss of my son. I'm deep in the process of grieving, and I'm told that it usually takes months—or even a few years—to come to a healthy place of recovery. There is no such thing as "getting over it." There is only learning to "live with it." My tears and sadness are actually signs that I'm moving forward in my grief.

There will be times when I'm not myself. For now my perceptions and judgments are unsettled. I feel like a 9.5 earthquake has jolted apart everything that was once connected, and I'm in the midst of the rubble that's settling. I'm not sure what I'll be like when the dust clears, so I may not always make sense to you. Thank you ahead of time for being patient with me.

More than anything else, I need your acceptance. I don't expect you to fully understand what I'm going through. I'd love it if you'd listen and just be with me. There is no right or wrong way to move through grief, and there is no time-table or schedule for how I should be doing.

Please don't let me run away. If you see me doing this, confront me, and hold me account-able to what I'm saying right now—that I want

*to choose to keep living life, and to keep trusting
God no matter what.*

*I need your prayers, and I need your attention
for months to come. I'll soon come to a place where
I want to listen to your own stories that will serve
to strengthen me.*

*I know that I'll not always feel as I do right now.
One day I'll feel like I'm breathing fresh air again.
Pray that that day will come soon, but not before
I've learned what I can from the smog of this
suffering.*

*Thank you for your love and support. It is a
priceless gift that you care for me.*

I love you all,
Sandy

Remember the relationship. Larry Yeagley, hospital
chaplain and counselor, describes a concept he learned
working with hundreds of grieving people. He discusses this need of people to "review and reconstruct"
in his book *Grief Recovery*. He describes how many
people have grasped the intellectual aspect of their
loved one's death, but in all other areas of their life
they are still "living" with the loved one. They continue to expect the spouse or child to meet them at
home, observing the familiar family routines.

In Yeagley's words:

*"In my early work with grieving people I urged
them to say good-bye to their relationship with
the lost. Many of these people resisted my
suggestion because they were still searching for
the person who was missing. They were putting
all their energy into preserving the relationship—
the opposite of what I was asking them to do."[1]*

Yeagley concludes that it's better early in the grieving process to review and reconstruct the total relationship. For many this is not only comforting but also starts the process of letting out feelings. Ultimately it can keep the grieving person from getting stuck midstream in grief.

> *When a loved one dies, the bereaved person wants to share with another person how worthwhile the loved one was. When that opportunity is not provided, there is an empty feeling inside. A choked-up sensation takes over, making future sharing of feelings difficult.*
>
> *Reviewing and reconstructing the relationship becomes repetitive. People say to me, "I must sound like a broken record. Aren't you bored with this?" I am very quick to let them know that the repetition is vital. How I feel isn't important. What the repetition is doing for them really matters.*[2]

I identify with what Yeagley says. In fact, it may be one of *the* most important things that was necessary to my first movements forward into healthy grieving. Telling my own story has helped me process my pain and more easily do the letting go that is so necessary.

* * * * *

Later on in your grieving process:

Look for local support groups. Beginning to share your story with others—and in return listening to their stories—is the start of returning to the ebb and flow of life. But avoid comparing your loss with anyone else's— each experience is unique.

Get involved in helping others. There is no "right time" to start reaching out, but if you withdraw and postpone this step indefinitely, you'll bog down in your grief and delay the growth that awaits you.

Do simple, everyday things for someone else who needs a helping hand—drive a senior to the shopping center; do housework for a shut-in; watch a single mom's children for her on a weekend afternoon; visit a sick friend in the hospital; read to a blind teenager. You may be surprised to discover that you benefit as much as—or even more than—the recipient of your kindness.

Create memory traditions. Find some special way to create traditions of memory around holiday times, birthdays, and other special family events. Our family has created several traditions to honor Trevor.

At Christmas, we light a candle in memory of Trevor and continue to each write a few lines to him in a journal.

Each year on the anniversary of Trevor's death I go to the hospital where he died and visit the nurses who cared for him. I take them the M & M candies that Trevor used to pass out.

I also send thank-you notes to Trevor's doctors, letting them know I'll not forget their expert care and concern for us.

Do something commemorative in memory of your loved one. At Trevor's school the faculty and students planted a beautiful young tree, surrounded by a brick flower bed, and placed a commemorative plaque in the school hallway. You might want to begin a memorial fund to serve others in need.

When my editor, Pat Horning Benton, lost her mother,

the family asked that monetary contributions be given to a special fund at *Insight* magazine, where Pat was an associate editor. The magazine sponsored a writing contest and awarded prizes from the fund. This helped to identify good new writers.

Celebrate those who are with you. I had to re-define family. It took time for me to accept the reality of the changed look and number of our family. It took time to stop looking for Trevor, as if he'd just gone away to camp for a while. I can now hold him in my heart while knowing that my family is complete—with those of us who are together now. Love those who are with you, and feel their love in return. The love of the one who is missing will flow between you.

Choose to love again! To open your heart and soul in love for another—and then have the beloved taken— feels like being squashed by a steamroller. For a long time I was cautious of loving that deeply again. But I now understand that I didn't lose Trevor—I gained him! When we truly love, it is always gain. To decide to pull ourselves into a shell and not venture out again is only to experience further loss.

Find outlets to express yourself. Redecorate, do crafts, pursue your musical interests, begin writing. Develop new interests, and learn new skills. Take up gardening, learn a new language, take an adult-ed class, read a good book. Do something you've always wanted to do, but always found a reason not to.

Take action on unresolved issues, or let them go. The action may be simple: making a phone call; writing a letter; but the release of resolution can be enormous.

Accept change in others. Understand that others have been changed by your loss as well. Family and friends each had relationships to your loved one, and they are struggling for the "dust" to settle for themselves as well.

When Trevor died I wasn't the only one who experienced great loss and sorrow. The lives of everyone connected to Trevor—father, siblings, grandparents, uncles and aunts, cousins, friends, teachers—are now changed forever. Others may not have changed in the same ways I have, and I have to respect their decisions about how they relate to loss.

Say good-bye. I remember working as a facilitator with a problem-solving team at my hospital. The group had experienced the suicide of one of their teammates. As the weeks went on I noticed that they were agitated with one another, out of focus, and off track from their goals.

One day I opened the group meeting by saying, "We're going to spend today saying good-bye to Donna (not her real name). At first they were skeptical, but as they began to talk about their feelings regarding her death, you could see the tension crumble. Tears flowed, apologies abounded, and each one wrote a good-bye letter to Donna, which they kept. The next few weeks were the highlight of their performance together.

It helped me so much to write a good-bye letter to Trevor. It affirmed my deep sorrow over missing him, my unending love for him, and my eager anticipation of our reunion someday. Then I tied the letter on a ribbon at the end of a helium balloon, and let it go at his graveside. Here's what I said to him:

My forever little son,
I sit here by your grave today, just three months

since you mercifully fell to sleep. My mind is in a fog, and my heart aches from missing you. As a young mother I never dreamed that I would know such pain. But neither did I imagine such a love. You will forever be a part of me. The love that you so graciously gave me burns brightly in me. You and I said that because we love God and God lives in our hearts, we would never really be apart from each other.

You talked about how hard this would be for me—and you were oh, so right! I miss your sweet smile, dancing green eyes and giggly laugh. I miss singing together. I miss your big hugs, so freely given to everyone. I remember how you smiled big one day in the hospital, with food in your mouth, and said to the nurse, "I love my mom— she's the best!" I miss your love for life, and the way you saw the best in everyone. And I miss the strength and inspiration you were to me, even while facing such a scary unknown.

I promised you that other people would learn of your faith and courage, and you smiled big— even through your pain. And so I commit to your memory right here that I will write or tell your story wherever God leads me. I will continue to strive to be the kind of person that you saw me to be. What a blessed mom I am to have had you in my life! I have not lost you, but rather I have gained you—immeasurably.

I can't have a person-to-person relationship with you now, and so, as I release this balloon, I am letting you go. But I will cherish the memories of you, and the echoes of your voice, until Jesus comes, this ground breaks open, and these aching arms hold you once again. You said you will be looking for me, and I promise you, you will find me.

Thank you, thank you, Trevie, for all you have taught me. Because of how you touched my life, I will never be the same. As I whispered in your ear those last two sleepful days of your life, "I will always, always love you."

Until we meet again,
Mom

I'm still suffering the separation from Trevor, but *all* life is a gift from God, and I am most assuredly a richer person for the life Trevor shared with me.

Praise God—He is my Counselor and Comforter, and He enables me to reach beyond myself and bring comfort to someone else who is hurting.

Chapter Sixteen

Helping Adults in Loss

". . .weep with them that weep."
—Romans 12: 15, KJV

**"Praise be to the God and Father of our Lord
Jesus Christ, the Father of compassion and
the God of all comfort, who comforts us in all
our troubles, so that we can comfort those
in any trouble with the comfort we ourselves
have received from God."**
—2 Corinthians 1:3-4, NIV

Sometimes when I've had a hard day, my 6-year-old daughter crawls up onto my lap, wraps her arms around my neck and says, "I love you, Mommy." As her spirit responds to the ache in mine, she ministers to me. She doesn't ask me questions, or give me advice on how I could've made better choices that day, nor does she try to change my feelings. She just comes and sits with me and holds me. That's more therapy than a month of counseling sessions.

I think God's greatest miracle is that He transposes His spirit in us, so that we become His arms and hands extended to one another. He commissions us—more than that, He *enables* us—to bear each other's sorrows as well as joys. He risks being misunderstood because He entrusts His work to us—you and me—who can only vaguely convey

His grace through our imperfections.

Surely our greatest evidence of evil is our inhumanity towards others. And our crowning evidence of good is unconditional compassion—compassion in action. When we truly *care with commitment* it comes back to us tenfold and we are brought into unity and transformed into the image of God.

With these thoughts in mind, let's reflect on ways we can give help that is truly healing. But be prepared—you must be willing to be changed, for you will inevitably be changed as a result of really caring for another.

* * * * *

When Trevor died there initially was a deluge of phone calls, cards, and practical assistance. Such is usually the case as friends rally around the freshly wounded. But a couple of months later, the grieving person can feel like a social outcast. No one calls, no one writes. Life has moved on for those not living with the loss every day. There can be an overwhelming sense of isolation.

Those who are grieving need comfort on a regular basis, particularly in the first year. They need to be able to retell their story and reconstruct events and feelings. They need to know that others have not forgotten.

The two ways I was truly respected on my journey through pain were having friends and loved ones who were liberal with ongoing support, and being allowed to have my own pain without pressure to "get out of it."

Because we're each unique, we experience loss and deal with our emotions differently. With the loss of a child, each parent will grieve in his or her own way. One may need separateness to process internally, while the other needs to be physically and emotionally connected to the spouse in order to maintain a sense of comfort. It takes great self-control to maintain respect for the other's style of coping.

One of the most powerful ways of demonstrating your acceptance and understanding is in providing healing communication. This is called *reflective listening*, or *mirroring*. You listen for the emotional content behind the message being shared and reflect/rephrase it back to the speaker in an empathetic way in your own words. This manner of listening causes the speaker to feel understood and accepted.

My mom's mother developed Alzheimer's a few years ago and has progressively deteriorated. As this book goes to press, 90-year-old grandma is under the care of hospice, and not expected to live long. These last few years have been very difficult for my mom, since she's been daily involved with meeting Grandma's needs.

Read the following example of reflective listening out loud, and experience the validation and compassionate caring that it demonstrates:

Me: Hi, Mom. How are you doing today?

Mom: Oh, I guess I'm doing okay.

Me: So, you're doing okay then?

Mom: As well as I can be with what's going on with your grandmother.

Me: Mom, it sounds as if it's really hard to watch Grandma have such a difficult time.

Mom: (sound of tears) We were just starting to really enjoy each other when this disease took over.

Me: This is so hard because you and Grandma were beginning to get closer.

Mom: It just doesn't seem fair.

Me: And so you're angry and sad because this has happened and you wish you had more time to enjoy her.

Mom: That's right; you really understand how I feel.

Me: Well, I love you, Mom, and I know if this were happening to you and me, I'd be devastated.

Mom: Honey, why don't we get together and talk some more soon? . . .

Did I give my opinion of what I thought my mother should do, or how she could stop feeling the way she did? Before understanding this profound way of communicating, I would often try to get the person out of her pain, and help her feel better. Doing so actually made light of her feelings, and made her feel that my primary goal was to *fix* her—not to *understand* her.

We're commissioned by God to "Love one another" and "Bear one another's burdens." There are no prerequisites for being a comforter other than a willing spirit. May God abundantly bless you as you prayerfully consider how to be the most helpful.

Here are some suggestions, most of which are taken from my own experience of what was most helpful to me. I think you'll find at least some of them useful as you communicate with those who are experiencing loss.

PRACTICAL WAYS TO HELP OTHERS:

You'll need to begin by becoming familiar with the grieving person's situation and needs. Decide what you'd be willing to do, recognizing that you can't and shouldn't do it all. Contact the person and offer specific help, starting with the most difficult job. If the person rejects your initial offer, suggest something else. Be mindful that if the loss occurred in a family, the whole family has needs, including the children.

Usually if you ask the person to let you know if the family needs help, she won't. If you ask her to come up with something specific you could do to help, she won't be able to think of anything. She won't want to bother you, and she isn't able to focus on the family's practical needs. So just step in (gently, of course!), choose something, and do it! Watch for signs if you think you might be intruding, and back off if your friend feels uncomfortable.

Offer to be responsible (or coordinate a team effort) for one or more of these areas:

- Deliver complete, ready-to-eat dinners each evening. You might organize a team of families to cover two to four weeks of meals.

- Provide weekly housecleaning services for at least a month. Organize friends to share the load or hire (and pay for!) a professional cleaning service.

- Do yard work. In addition to mowing the lawn, friends (or a professional yard service) could also plant flowers and weed and feed the garden.

- Clean and maintain vehicles. (I read about one friend who called and offered to detail the family car so they'd have a sparkling vehicle the day of the memorial service.)

- Care for pets, especially if they need veterinary care or time-consuming grooming.

- Provide transportation, especially if out-of-town family and friends are coming for the funeral or memorial service.

- Run errands and do grocery shopping.

- Provide temporary financial assistance to meet the extra demands of a terminal illness and burial.

- Offer to include the children in special outings with your own family.

- Provide child care so the parents can go out or have some quiet, personal time.

- Assist with bill-paying, banking, and other business affairs.

- Make difficult phone calls, or write letters and thank-you notes.

- Offer to assume church responsibilities or find replacements for several weeks.

Help implement a commemorative project. For example, if the family wants to plant a memorial tree or garden, work with the nursery or a landscaper to get cost estimates and come up with a plan of action. If the project is a large one, recruit other volunteers to help with some of the work.

Have a plan to send a card or note frequently. Write each week for a month, then each month for a year, and then on anniversary dates such as birthdays and the date of death. This ongoing support will not go unnoticed!

Talk with the bereaved person about the one who died. Listen with understanding. Share your own memories of the deceased. Your empathy, understanding and respect will do much to assist the bereaved in knowing that his grief is normal and healthy.

Create a "memory scrapbook" of the one who died.

I can't begin to tell you what an invaluable treasure this can be. During their regular weekly Bible study time, a group of women from my church spent four of their meetings putting together a wonderful picture album of Trevor and surprised me with it.

Create a video compilation of the one who died. Your videos doubtless captured shared experiences that will help the bereaved smile and laugh and remember the good times you all shared.

Pay for a weekly massage for one month. For those who like massages, this is a greatly appreciated gift.

Pay for a trip for the bereaved—when he or she is ready to get away. Depending upon financial ability, such a gift could be a weekend getaway at the ocean or a trip across the country to visit their children and grandchildren.

Be patient! You'll hear the same story over and over again by the grieving person. It will have the same details, the same tears. In her book *Beyond Grief*, Carol Staudacher encourages potential comforters to talk about how the one who died enriched the lives of others, but then also to talk to the survivor about the interests he or she has—gardening, cooking, local politics, church activities—to help keep the sparks of these interests alive in the survivor. In this way, you validate the past, but you let the survivor know that there will be a future with these same interests in it.

Give the gift of touch. It has been said that we all need ten hugs a day just for emotional "maintenance," and more when we're under stress. Clinical studies have shown that caring touch lowers blood pressure and heart rate. Be sensitive to the fact that not everyone may be comfortable with the measure of touch you give. Don't hesitate to offer it, but proceed according to the cues of the griever.

Even if you're having trouble finding something useful to do or say, don't withdraw. Have you ever felt like you wanted to help but didn't know what to say? You're not alone; we all struggle with this issue, but it *is* possible to minister verbally to others in a way that is healing. Most importantly, don't withdraw from those who are grieving. Just your silent presence may be the most needed gift of all.

Here are some suggestions on dos and don'ts:

Things To Avoid:
. . ."Is there anything I can do to help?" or "Let me know if I can do anything." People flooded with grief may not know what they need or want. It takes too much energy to ask. They don't want to bother you.

. . .trying to minimize their pain with comments such as: "Well, at least you have two other children," "You're strong; you'll get over it soon," "God must love you a lot to trust you with so much pain." Although there's truth in these statements, when someone is hurting these comments make them feel as if their personal feelings are not important. The bereaved need to have pain acknowledged.

. . .using statements that have *should* or *shouldn't* in them: "You *shouldn't* feel that way," "You *should* be glad that he was in your life at all." This is a punishing way to talk to people who are hurting.

. . .offering spiritual clichés or Bible quotes. Don't remind the bereaved of how much stronger they'll be as a result of this experience. Intellectual truths are not a source of comfort in the acute stages of grief—and *no one* of us has all the answers!

Things To Offer:

. . .focusing on specific things you can do to help. Look around for something that needs to be done, then jump in and do it.

. . .understanding statements such as, "This must be very hard for you," "I hurt for you during this very difficult time," "I know how special he was to you," "I'll miss him, too." If you're not sure what to say, it's better to be honest and say, "I honestly don't know what to say, but I want to be here for you."

. . .encouraging the bereaved to talk with someone they trust—which could be you if you listen in a comforting way! Suggest they keep a journal of their feelings. There are no right or wrong feelings, but there are healthy ways of processing them.

. . .comfort the bereaved by saying, "Yes, life is unfair, and what happened to you doesn't make sense." Your perception of this sad event will not be the same as theirs. Even their own perception will change over time. You don't have to be in agreement with someone to offer your support and comfort. You *can* share concepts or verses that were comforting to you at a specific time in your life. This offers a vision of hope.

. . .and finally, *pray with* the griever. Take the time to enter into prayer for that person while you are with them (or over the phone). However, respect their desire to decline at this time without passing judgment on their eternal destiny!

Many people may appear to be "losing their faith" after they've suffered a great loss. Even the most spiritually surrendered believer has to struggle through grief. He or she also has to sit down and mourn for a time. Each person will do it differently, yet each and every one will need comforting.

God has touched my life most directly through the loving hands and earnest prayers of my brothers and sisters in Christ. As God dwells in us—and as we listen to His leading—we'll be able to lift each other up in loving comfort and support and transcend our tragedies together. We'll eagerly anticipate that Great Day when "...God shall wipe away all tears" (Revelation 21:4, *KJV)* and we'll live forever in the fellowship that we've begun here on earth.

Chapter Seventeen

Helping Children in Loss

**"We can't know why the lily has so brief a time
to bloom in the warmth of sunlight's kiss upon its
face, before it folds its fragrance in and bids the
world goodnight to rest its beauty in a gentler place.
But we can know that nothing that is loved
is ever lost, and no one who has ever touched
a heart can really pass away, because
some beauty lingers on in each memory
of which they've been a part."**
—Ellen Brenneman

Without a doubt the most difficult loss in my life—and
that of others I've talked with—has been the death of a
child. With that loss goes a multitude of cherished hopes
and dreams.

We acknowledge this difficulty for adults, but what about
the children? What about the child facing imminent death?
What about the children who have lost someone vital in
their lives—a sibling, a parent, a grandparent? How do we
best help them through their individual journeys of grief?
This chapter is difficult to write, but I think it's important for
me to share some of the insights our family gained.

When I was in my pediatric rotation in nurses' training,
I thought that would be my area of specialization. But after
spending time at Children's Hospital in Los Angeles and

watching the terminally ill patients, I just couldn't do it. Nursing kids who were in pain or dying was very difficult, and my hat is off to those who've answered the call to minister to these children. I will forever be deeply grateful to the nurses at Santa Barbara Cottage Hospital Pediatrics Unit who became as family to us, ministering lovingly to Trevor, and grieving along with us.

It's important to tell children right away that they're not expected to live. This was true with Trevor, and the reading I've done since bears it out. Hope and pray always, but prepare for the separation. Thank God for the hope that our separation is temporary, and we need not panic!

A terminal illness is such a difficult time. The whole family is trying to do several contradictory things at the same time—get closer, let go, and still maintain normalcy. Just getting through each day is an incredible juggling match.

Parents need to be with their child as much as possible during this final event of his life. The child is usually not as afraid of dying as he is of being alone or being in pain. He wants to feel protected. The child also needs permission to let go and rest. Assure him that he's done his best and that you're proud of him. He needs to know that everyone—himself and his family—will be okay.

Closure is important. Let the child do whatever he needs to—complete projects, call people, write letters—to bring closure to his issues and with the people closest to him. Encourage him to talk about things that have been important to him, and memories that are fondest. Stay busy during the day with reading, crafts, and visits with loved ones. Allow as much visitation as his strength will permit. This is an important time for all—to connect with what really matters in this life.

If possible have the child do things that will be of strength to you later. These things have created a rainbow of remembrance for me; they are priceless treasures. Consider these options for the child:

- Draw or color pictures for different family members
- Write letters (or dictate if the child is too young or too sick to write)
- Talk into a tape recorder or video camera
- Take pictures
- Make a scrapbook together
- Make a clay impression of the child's hand
- Clip a lock of hair and save it

The terminal illness and death of a child impacts other children, especially those closest to the child who has died. I felt a special burden for Trevor's classmates.

About two weeks after Trevor died, I made arrangements with his teacher to visit his first-grade classroom. I felt drawn to communicate with the children, and wondered, too, if they might be wanting to connect with their feelings and memories of their friend. I'd made a few notes for a discussion I'd planned, but I didn't expect the rich feast they fed me! They were eager to pour their little hearts out.

I began by thanking them for their prayers for Trevor. Those prayers had helped to make him strong and brave and helped him trust Jesus more through such a difficult time. I briefly explained the type of tumor Trevor had, and the basics of what had been done for him, and that everything was done that could have been done.

I let them know I'd come to give them a chance to ask questions and to share in remembering Trevor. I let them know that I was very sad, too, and that it was okay to feel sad or angry or confused. I wanted them to know that it wouldn't bother me to talk about it. And I reminded them that God understood perfectly because He had watched His Son Jesus die for us, and He had the feelings we did.

My first question to them was, "What was Trevor like?"

They couldn't wait to talk about how they remembered him! I had tears in my eyes as they responded.

> "Friendly."
>
> "Always happy."
>
> "Cute!" the girls said.
>
> "Helpful."
>
> "Everybody's friend."

One little boy, who I knew was not very popular, said shyly, "Not many kids pay attention to me, but Trevor was always nice to me, and he shared his lunch with me."

We all had tears—teacher too—as we shared a common bond in our memories of a treasured friend and the huge sense of his loss.

Next I asked them to tell me what feelings they were having about Trevor's death.

> "Confused, because we prayed for him to get well and he died anyway."
>
> "Sad."
>
> "Angry that I didn't get to say good-bye."
>
> "Could we have done more?"
>
> "Glad that he was my friend."

We talked about how those feelings were normal—and healthy—and it was important to talk about them with a trusted grownup.

Then I asked them, "What would you like to say to Trevor right now?" And they began to answer.

> "I miss you, Trevor."
>
> "I can't wait to see you in heaven."

"I'm so sorry this happened to you."

We discussed what the Bible says about death—that it's like a sleep while we wait for Jesus to come and call us awake at the resurrection. I told them that although we couldn't talk with Trevor right now, sometimes it was helpful to write a good-bye letter, so we could say all the things to our hearts that we wished we could say to Trevor. I reminded them that the love and friendship he shared with us will always be with us.

Then I asked them, "Should we stop trusting God because Trevor died?" And they all answered, "No way!"

They reminded me that God doesn't always answer the way we wish for, but that His plans are always the best. Nevertheless, we were all honest enough to say that we didn't understand God's ways, and that it didn't make sense now, but that someday in heaven we would understand perfectly. God loved Trevor more than we did, and what He allowed flows out of love and wisdom.

We sang together one of Trevor's favorite songs, "Walk in the Light of the Lord." And they sang their little hearts out.

I ended by asking them what they were looking forward to doing in heaven. And they answered,

"Seeing Jesus and Trevor."

"Flying."

"Breathing under water." (I especially liked that one!)

We closed our eyes and imagined what heaven would look like, smell like, and feel like. And mostly we talked about wanting to be there, and about how Trevor would be looking for all of us.

I experienced true community with those children that day. With the open invitation to talk about something painful, they spoke with honesty and compassion. Our time together made them feel heard and understood. I cried all the way home because of the gift they had given me.

To this day many of those children—now in fifth grade—have Trevor's first-grade picture taped to their desk where they can see it daily.

This experience emphasized to me the importance of helping children process their grief in ways appropriate to their age and loss.

Two of the best resources I've found are books entitled *Helping Children Grieve* by Theresa Huntley, and *When a Loved One Dies. . .A Family Guide to Helping Children Cope*, which was prepared by the San Diego Children's Project and is published by the American Cancer Society. If you're anticipating loss in your family—or classroom—get these excellent resources as soon as possible.

*When a Loved One Dies. . .*covers such important topics as age-specific descriptions of children's perceptions of death, preparing a child for the death of a loved one, telling a child that a loved one has died, common childhood reactions to grief, typical questions children ask, how and when the grieving child should return to school, and discussing the spiritual aspects of death. One of the best sections is reprinted below:

Guidelines for Helping Children Cope with Death

1. Tell your children immediately when the death occurs.

2. Explain the death in terms that your children can understand. Use correct terms such as "die," "died," "dying," and "dead". . .

3. Express your own feelings about the death openly. It's okay for your children to see you angry, upset, crying, relieved, etc. This allows them to see what you are really feeling. It also gives them permission to express the same feelings.

4. Do not force feelings of grief. Your children should be allowed to express their feelings naturally in *their own way*, and in *their own time.*

5. Really listen to what your children are asking or saying. To understand what they are expressing, you may need to ask further questions.

6. Maintain routines as much as possible. It is helpful for your children to remain in familiar places (their rooms, their home) and with familiar loved ones. Even though a death has occurred, the children's lives go on.

7. Your children may need to see or touch the body to help them understand the reality of death.

8. Saying good-bye is important for children. Children may wish to do the following:

   • Talk to the loved one who has died.

   • Write a letter or draw a picture.

   • Place a picture or favorite toy in the casket or in the grave.

   • Place flowers on the grave at a later date.

   • Complete a project the children were working on with the loved one before death occurred.

9. Even though a loved one has died, reassure your children that the loved one still remains in your hearts and in your memories.

10. Maintain an openness to discussing the loved one who has died and the subject of death in general. There is no inappropriate time or place to talk about death and dying.

11. Be sensitive to your own feelings and needs. Take care of yourself.[1]

My experience with my own children through the loss of their brother was an uncharted path. They've experienced many of the emotions described in *When a Loved One Dies. . .* The journey has been made more healing through open and honest communication, by never making the topic of Trevor or his death a closed subject. He continues to be a member of our family, and although physically absent, he is very much alive inside us.

We had only a few days to prepare Trevor's siblings for his impending death. Taryn was only two and wasn't really aware of what was happening. She only knew something was making those she loved incredibly sad. Todd, however, was 10 years old, and it was a difficult time for him.

Todd understood the finality of Trevor's death. It was double pain for me to watch his confusion and woundedness. But it would have been far worse not to have talked about it. I followed his cues as to his readiness to talk, but I also let him see my tears and hear me say I didn't have the answers, but was choosing to trust God anyway.

We let Todd make the decision about when to rearrange the room he'd shared with Trevor for more than three years. He came to me about three weeks after Trevor's death and said he wanted to begin to move his brother's things out. I had him help me put some of Trevor's clothes and favorite things away in tubs. While we did this most difficult task together, I gently reminisced about funny events and good times I recalled the brothers having together.

Todd was able to express that he missed getting up in the middle of the night with Trevor and sneaking into the kitchen to get a snack. And there were all those nights they'd just talk and laugh while in their beds.

Soon after this transitional event of moving Trevor's things out, Todd made decisions about how to decorate this room that was now all his.

I don't think Todd has done his grief work yet. Many specialists say that it isn't until children are in their later teens that they can feel at a level that allows them to truly grieve.

* * * * *

Talking is important for the child who is dying. In those last few days Trevor and I talked a lot about heaven, and I encouraged him to ask questions—any questions. Mostly he wanted to make sure that we were going to be all right. Sometimes tears became our only communication, and we just held each other, trying to stop the passing of time.

Those final 360 hours became the most bitter, and yet the sweetest, time of my life. Trevor lent me such joy and strength in those final days. Together we got a clear picture of our blessed future—reunited, someday soon!

Perspectives

All the way my Savior leads me;
What have I to ask beside?
Can I doubt His tender mercy,
Who through life has been my guide?
Heavenly peace, divinest comfort,
Here by faith in Him to dwell;
For I know whate'er befall me,
Jesus doeth all things well.

All the way my Savior leads me;
Cheers each winding path I tread;
Gives me grace for every trial,
Feeds me with the living bread;
Though my weary steps may falter,
And my soul athirst may be,
Gushing from the Rock before me,
Lo, a spring of joy I see.

All the way my Savior leads me;
O the fullness of His love!
Perfect rest to me is promised
In my Father's house above;
When I wake to life immortal,
Wing my flight to realms of day,
This my song through endless ages,
Jesus led me all the way.
—Fanny J. Crosby

Epilogue

"Now I know in part; then I shall know fully. . ."
—1 Corinthians 13:12, NIV

As I come to the completion of this manuscript, I'm experiencing the frustration of coming to the end, yet having so much more to say! God continues to reveal more of Himself to me daily. There are colors on the landscape of my life that I've never seen before.

Four years after the death of Trevor, my feelings parallel those of Gerald L. Sittser, a Christian college professor who lost his mother, his wife, and his daughter all in one tragic accident. Here's how he describes his feelings:

After three years. . .there is a significant difference now. The sorrow I feel has not disappeared, but it has been integrated into my life as a painful part of a healthy whole. Initially, my loss was so overwhelming to me that it was the dominant emotion—sometimes the only emotion I had. I felt like I was staring at the stump of a huge tree that had just been cut down in my backyard. That stump, which sat all alone, kept reminding me of the beloved tree that I had lost. I could think of nothing but that tree. Every time I looked out the window, all I could see was that stump. Eventually, however, I decided to do something about it. I landscaped my backyard, reclaiming it once again as my own. I decided to keep the stump there, since it was both too big and too precious to remove. Instead of getting rid of it, I worked around it. I planted shrubs, trees, flowers, and grass. I laid out a brick pathway and built two benches. Then I watched everything grow. Now, three years later, the stump remains, still reminding me of the beloved tree I lost. But the stump is surrounded by a beautiful garden of blooming flowers and growing trees and lush grass. Likewise, the sorrow I feel remains, but I have tried to create a landscape around the loss so that what was once ugly is now an integral part of a larger, lovely whole.[1]

I have been asked to tell Trevor's story in many places—from churches to women's groups to television broadcasts. Many people have written or spoken to me about how it has helped them face their own loss and continue their process of healing. We connect in our brokenness, yet rejoice together in the comfort God gives us, and the blessed hope of our heavenly reunion.

Now I am more able to recognize His work in the lives of others. As I wrote this, a dear friend lost her life in a head-on crash, caused by a 16-year-old drunk driver who had just received his driver's license the day before.

My friend lay quiet, without brain waves, for a few days. Then her husband had to make the torturous decision to turn off life support. In the midst of his overwhelming sadness, he made it clear to the community that he holds no animosity to the one whose carelessness caused such a tragedy that changed his life forever. Because both he and his wife had chosen to trust God with all of their lives, this man will not be moved!

Loss robs us of our props. We *choose* whether to be enlarged or diminished by the loss. We experience what

C. S. Lewis calls a "severe mercy"—a mystery that we'll study throughout eternity. We are changed, and we begin to be grateful for that. We redefine "miracle" and "normal." We plunge deep and we soar high—and it is only because of God's amazing grace that we survive at all.

If you have not yet given your life completely to our ever-loving God, I invite you to now. There's no set protocol, just a simple choice to let Him be Lord. When you do, your life won't be the same. You'll still have problems and disappointments and grief, but you'll also have the quiet confidence that God is in control.

As Max Lucado writes:

His [God's] goal is not to make you happy. His goal is to make you His. His goal is not to get you what you want; it is to get you what you need. . .God wants to get you home safely.[2]

Someday in heaven I want you to tell me *your* story! We'll gather together with all our dear ones and sing praises to the One who sustained us. As we sit in His loving presence, He'll reveal His divine purposes in each of our earthly journeys.

Until we have that grand reunion, my prayer is that you will let God hold you, help you, and heal you.

Sandy Wyman Richert
Bakersfield, California
July, 1997

*"He has sent me to bind up the brokenhearted,
to proclaim freedom for the captives
and release for the prisoners. . .
to comfort all who mourn,
and provide for those who grieve in Zion—
to bestow on them a crown of beauty instead of ashes,
the oil of gladness instead of mourning,
and a garment of praise instead of a spirit of despair."*

—*Isaiah 61:1-3, NIV*

We Remember Trevor

A collection of memories
from those who knew Trevor best

"I remember that Trevor had something growing in his head and he had to die.

"I remember that when he was sick I used to climb up on his special bed, and he would feed me French fries and ketchup.

"He is still my brother; right now he is waiting for Jesus to come and wake him up, and we can be together forever in heaven.

"I remember that he loved me a lot!"

—Taryn Richert, age 5, sister

"My brother Trevor and I had a few big differences. The biggest one was that he loved to draw and read and stay inside, and I loved to play sports and do things outside. I also remember at night after our mom and dad went to sleep, we would have pillow fights in our room until one of us started crying or we got into trouble. Also during the night we would get up and go out to the kitchen and eat cream-filled oatmeal cookies. I miss him."

—Todd Richert, age 14, brother

"I remember Trevor as a vivacious, energetic child. He would bound into the classroom every morning ready for the day. He was full of anticipation to see who was in class that day. Trevor went from child to child anxious to learn what they had done since leaving school the day before, as he shared their joys and listened to their 6-year-old sorrows with a passionate heart.

"Trevor was especially thrilled if we were to create masterpieces with clay, or to paint during art time. Trevor also loved to draw. He could sit for great lengths of time if he simply had a pencil and paper before him. . .

"What I remember most about Trevor, though, was the way his face lit up when he talked of his family. He especially liked to tell about his new baby sister, Taryn. His eyes brightened and his face glowed as he shared tales of Taryn with the class. Our class was lucky to have been blessed with Trevor's presence for that one special year. . ."

—*Diane Wilcock, Kindergarten teacher*

"Trevor never walked—he ran, plunging into each day with a passion, dancing on his toes. 'There's always a song in my head,' he would say. I would nod and say, 'Me too,' and we would sing together. . .

"I think the tree house was his favorite place. I can still see him up there, whispering to Kimily [my granddaughter], playing with Legos, or eating a snack. He lent joy to my life.

"But the greatest joy was when he told his mom and dad he wanted to see Jesus, because then I knew he was saved. I'm longing for the day when Jesus comes and Trevor, Kimily, and I can have tea parties at the Tree of Life."

—*Ruth Goodman, SS Teacher*

"I remember Trevor as being kind, thoughtful of others, willing to help; and I also remember him as being my best friend. I think part of the reason we became best friends is because every day after kindergarten, he would come over to my grandma's house with me and we would play in the tree house or play on the merry-go-round in the backyard. After we were done playing, we would usually go inside and watch a movie. Then around 2:15, my grandma, Trevor, and I would go back to the big school so Trevor could ride the school bus home. That happened every day until we started first grade.

"Sometimes Trevor wore a hat to school because he didn't have time to brush his hair. It didn't work out very well. Especially since boys can't wear hats inside the classroom. Well, after he took it off, Miss Issa [the first grade teacher], seeing how messy his hair was, would comb it for him.

"I don't really remember a lot since it happened over three years ago, but I do remember that never once while Trevor had the brain tumor did he stop believing in God. Sometimes when I get sad about him, it helps to know that since he never stopped believing in God, I will see him again some day in heaven."

—*Kimily Gerking, age 11, Trevor's friend*

"Trevor arrived as a first-grade student in my classroom. He was always pleasant, even when he was being disciplined. There were many mornings when he came walking into my classroom with unkempt hair. . .and without his homework. He would shrug and say to me, 'Whoops, I forgot my homework again!' Even though I wanted to reprimand him, I found his good-morning smile disarming. So I would just give him a hug, ask him to remember it the next time. . .then comb his hair. That was Trevor. Always living on the edge.

"During the spring parent/teacher conferences I met with his mother, Sandy. I shared with her that Trevor was beginning to settle down and concentrate. As I was saying that, the thought struck me and I continued, 'Come to think of it,

I wonder if that's good; maybe he's sick or something.'

"About a week later during a dinner conversation his parents mentioned that Trevor had been seeing double, even having to close one eye in order to watch television or read a book. They had made an appointment for a doctor to examine him the very next week.

"When his mother came to school to pick up Todd after taking Trevor to his doctor's appointment, I went out to the van to see Trevor. I had a compelling urge to tell him I loved him. For some reason, I sensed that something terrible was about to happen to him, and I didn't want him to face whatever it was without knowing that he had touched my life, and that I cared about him. . .

"He never returned to my classroom. I visited him in the hospital and joined groups praying for his recovery. I took the entire class to his house for his birthday when he had returned home from the hospital for a short time. . .

"I was impressed that God had given Trevor a special ministry to his friends, demonstrating that the most important things in life are the people our lives touch. Because of this experience, I have learned two important lessons which I've incorporated into my teaching:

- The individual is more important than his accomplishments. Who he is is more important than what he does.

- Make the most out of every opportunity that life offers.

"Trevor used his seven years more abundantly than most of us do in seventy!
                    —*Intissar Issa, Trevor's first-grade teacher*

"We all have different memories of Trevor's last days; I remember like it was yesterday that day Sandy sat at his bedside in the hospital to tell him he had a brain tumor and might not have long to live. After some tears he spoke the words I still hear echoing in my heart, 'Well, at least I had 7 years; some people don't even have that.'

"My heart felt like breaking as I listened to my brave little nephew declare such acceptance of an event most of us would tremble at. He challenged my own view of death. . ."

—Stacey Wyman, aunt

"This is what of Trevor lives on in me: his smile. He was more often with his smile than without it. And that smile would disarm me. There was a spirit within that smile that could shift my mood, open my heart, and cause me to remember how precious we all are. . .

"Trevor was 'an old soul'—he seemed to know and live, even at his young age, those principles and qualities of life that I am still working to develop. I find I talk about him often in my counseling work, using him as an example of living fully, joyfully, and from an open heart. May we all grow to know that kind of living before we leave this life."

—Scott Wyman, uncle

"Trevor Richert was a special patient from the get-go. He was surrounded by a love that would get him through the toughest ordeal, and yet his maturity and compassion for others seemed far beyond his years. It was as if he knew what lay ahead, and he was paving the road for all of us.

"I will never forget what a giving soul he was. Here I was, the care-giver, and every time I needed to leave his room he always made sure that my pocket was loaded with M & M's. While most kids covet and hide their candy stash, Trevor always gave his away. I know I will never meet another child like him."

—Julie LeBourveau, RN, Pediatrics
Santa Barbara Cottage Hospital

"You could sense it from your first meeting with him—Trevor was someone special. The bond between Trevor and Sandy was magical. There was little need for verbal exchange between them. They were truly kindred spirits. When Trevor's communications skills were poor due to his slurred speech [secondary to the tumor], Sandy could always understand him. He would try to encourage his little body to do a particular task, and Sandy would not only know what he was attempting to do, but why. There was complete understanding, trust and sharing between them."

—Sue McClellan, RN, Pediatrics
Santa Barbara Cottage Hospital

"Sweet Trevor, your hands would tremble, you could barely hold your head up—but you would always try again. Your voice had become weaker by your final hospitalization, your speech severely slurred, and you could no longer even sit or move without violent dizziness and vomiting. Yet your spirit never trembled. Your faith and hope in God's infinite plan went unquestioned. I remember your finding strength in prayer, and I remember how much that helped me, too. . .

"You were so weak, but your enthusiasm and courage were always evident. The calm of your spirit, your faith, and your commitment to your family were remarkable.

"I'll never forget your music, especially the tape with "Jump down, turn around, touch the ground and praise my Lord." How great it will be when we can all jump and dance to it in heaven someday!"

—Paralee Schmechel, RN, Pediatrics
Santa Barbara Cottage Hospital

To Todd and Taryn

Letters to my children

Dear Todd,

When I start to count my blessings, son, I always start with you. You were the first life I felt moving inside of me, and I have loved you ever since. Even then you were full of delightful energy!

When you were tiny I remember looking into your eyes and watching you look into mine. I wondered if you could already see that I was not always going to be a perfect mom. There would be times when I'd disappoint you, times when I'd be too strict—or not strict enough.

You are my firstborn, and because of that every parenting skill is tried on you first. I've never before been the mother of a 14-year-old. . .humor me.

I made many promises to you as a baby, but the only one I've really kept is this one—always to love you. I feel so lucky to be your mom! People often tell me how much you and I look alike. I hope that doesn't disturb you too deeply, 'cuz it makes me feel great!

Although I know what it's like to lose a son, I have no idea what it's like to lose a brother. You've been through a lot of loss for someone so young. It will affect your life—but it can make you stronger, just like deep roots make a tree able to withstand strong winds.

Don't run from your sad feelings, my son. The feelings of pain are part of the love you will always feel for Trevor. You two had your moments, but I know you loved him very much and he adored you. The life you had with him here—and the love you felt for him here—are part of you. That love will give you strength to press on and become what God plans for you to be here on earth. It will prepare you for a fantastic reunion with Trevor in heaven!

I've never told you this before, but the day after Trevor had the seizure in the hospital (and we all knew he was getting worse), he asked to see the family portrait. He reached out and touched each face in the picture—and it was your face that he touched first.

Please know this, Todd. Trevor was not the most loved child in the family because he died. If you had died, this book would have begun by telling your story. You and your little sister are here—and matter to me more than anything! I feel called to tell of my journey through the death of Trevor so that others who are in similar pain may be comforted.

I pray for you every day, my son, that you will know that God loves you no matter what and that your desire will be to let God lead in your life. Life will not always make sense or seem fair, but behind the scenes God is working it all out.

Thank you for the joy you bring to my life.

I love you, Todd.
Mom

Dearest Tiny Taryn,

We have called you Tiny Taryn since the day you came into the world weighing only 1 pound, 11 ounces. You had not been included in my "life's agenda," but sometimes the best things in life are unplanned!

I was so glad when I found out that I was going to have a baby girl! I'd been blessed with the two boys and looked forward to a lifetime of "boy things." Now I found myself happy about the prospect of also having "girl things" around. I thought every day about what you would be like. I didn't have as long to think about it as most pregnant moms have; at six and one-half months you had to be delivered by emergency surgery.

You were so tiny and weak those first few weeks. I was so afraid to love you because it would hurt more if something happened to you. But there was something so special about you that I admit it—I fell in love, hard!

You have been adored and loved by so many in your short five years. One of your biggest admirers was Trevor. He couldn't touch and kiss you enough. He read stories to you, sang songs to you, and bragged about you to his friends. No baby sister could have been more loved. When Trevor got sick and was away from home, he always wanted to know how you and Todd were doing. He missed you so much! While he was home those three weeks in a hospital bed in the living room, you used to crawl up onto his bed and sit with him. You would touch his face, and he would hug you. You were only two years old, but he let you color on his pages.

And when he knew he was going to die, he said, "Take special care of Taryn; she's so tiny!"

Taryn, even though you knew Trevor for only two short years, he is part of your life and always will be. The love he gave you will give you strength and courage—

forever. I love to hear you tell others, "I have two broth-ers. One is sleeping and waiting for Jesus to come, and then we'll be together again."

One day, about a year after Trevor died, I was look-ing at his pictures and crying. You climbed up onto my lap and said, "Mommy, are you sad because you miss Trevor?"

When I said, yes, you responded, "That's okay to be sad, Mommy, but we'll see him again!"

That's what I've been sharing in this book. Forty more years hasn't made me able to say it better than you did.

Taryn, I can't begin to tell you what a blessing you are in my life. You light up a room, and you have shed a bright light in my heart. I thank Jesus for you every day, and I pray that you will always let Jesus lead you. He is your best Friend.

I love you, Taryn
Mom

Comfort Texts

These texts have been of special comfort and strength to me. This is by no means an exhaustive listing of all of the texts of comfort and encouragement in the Bible. Be sure to add some of your own to the list!

"Cast thy burden upon the Lord,
and he shall sustain thee. . ."
—Psalm 55:22, KJV

"God is our refuge and strength,
a very present help in trouble.
Therefore will not we fear,
though the earth be removed,
and though the mountains be carried
into the midst of the sea. . ."
—Psalm 46:1-2, KJV

"Even though I walk through the valley
of the shadow of death,
I will fear no evil, for you are with me;
your rod and your staff, they comfort me."
—Psalm 23:4, NIV

"He that dwelleth in the secret place of the Most High
shall abide under the shadow of the Almighty."
—Psalm 91:1, KJV

"I know what it is to be in need, and I know what it is to have plenty. I have learned the secret of being content in any and every situation, whether well fed or hungry, whether living in plenty or in want. I can do everything through him who gives me strength."
—*Philippians 4:12-13, NIV*

"My flesh and my heart faileth:
but God is the strength of my heart,
and my portion forever."
—*Psalm 73:26, KJV*

". . .they that wait upon the Lord shall renew their strength;
they shall mount up with wings as eagles;
they shall run, and not be weary;
and they shall walk, and not faint."
—*Isaiah 40:31, KJV*

". . .he said to me, "My grace is sufficient for you,
for my power is made perfect in weakness."
—*2 Corinthians 12:9, NIV*

". . .when you lie down, you will not be afraid;
when you lie down, your sleep will be sweet."
—*Proverbs 3:24, NIV*

"Casting all your care upon him; for he careth for you."
—*1 Peter 5:7, KJV*

"He heals the brokenhearted and binds up their wounds."
—*Psalm 147:3, NIV*

". . .be content with what you have, because God has said,
'Never will I leave you; never will I forsake you.'"
—*Hebrews 13:5, NIV*

Suggested Reading

Austin, Bill. Wh*en God Has Put You On Hold: Living Productively in the Meantime*. Wheaton, IL: Tyndale House Publishers, Inc., 1986.

Barnes, M. Craig. *Yearning: Living Between How It Is & How It Ought to Be*. Downers Grove, IL: InterVarsity Press, 1991.

Becton, Randy. *Everyday Comfort: Readings for the First Month of Grief*. Grand Rapids, MI: Baker Books, Baker Book House, 1993.

Blunt, Kathie and Lilah Scalzo. *Someone I Love Died: An Activity Book for Children Experiencing the Loss of a Loved One*. Loma Linda, CA: Loma Linda Hospice, 1990.

Colgrove, Melba, Harold H. Bloomfield & Peter McWilliams. *How to Survive the Loss of a Love*. Los Angeles, CA: Prelude Press, 1991.

Crabb, Lawrence J., Jr. *Finding God*. Grand Rapids, MI: Zondervan Publishing House, 1993.

Dobson, James. *When God Doesn't Make Sense*. Wheaton, IL: Tyndale House Publishers, Inc., 1993.

Elliot, Elisabeth. *A Path Through Suffering*. Ann Arbor, MI: Vine Books, Servant Publications, 1990.

Faber, Rebecca. *A Mother's Grief Observed*. Wheaton, IL: Tyndale House Publishers, Inc., 1997.

Frankl, Viktor E. *Man's Search for Meaning*, 1984 edition. New York, NY: Washington Square Press, Simon & Schuster Inc., 1984.

Fry, Virginia Lynn. *Part of Me Died, Too: Stories of Creative Survival Among Bereaved Children and Teenagers*. New York, NY: Dutton Children's Books, Penguin USA, 1995.

Heatherley, Joyce Landorf. *Mourning Song*, rev. ed. Grand Rapids, MI: Fleming H. Revell, a division of Baker Book House Co., 1994.

Huntley, Theresa. *Helping Children Grieve: When Someone They Love Dies*. Minneapolis, MN: Augsburg Fortress, 1991.

Lenzkes, Susan. *When Life Takes What Matters: Devotions to Comfort You Through Crisis & Change*. Grand Rapids, MI: Discovery House Publishers, 1993.

—more

Lewis, C. S. *A Grief Observed.* New York, NY: Bantum Books published by arrangement with The Seabury Press, Inc., 1961.

Lucado, Max. A G*entle Thunder.* Dallas, TX: Word Publishing, 1995.

MacDonald, Gordon. *The Life God Blesses.* Nashville, TN: Thomas Nelson, Inc., Publishers, 1994.

Ogilvie, Lloyd J. *If God Cares, Why Do I Still Have Problems?* Waco, TX: Word Books, 1985.

Reeve, Pamela. Fai*th Is...* Sisters, OR: Multnomah Books, Questar Publishers, Inc., 1994.

Rizzo, Kay. *On Wings of Praise: How I found Real Joy in a Personal Friendship with God.* Hagerstown, MD: Review and Herald Publishing Association, 1996.

San Diego Children's Project. *When a Loved One Dies...* San Diego, CA: The American Cancer Society California, 1988.

Sittser, Gerald L. *A Grace Disguised: How the Soul Grows Through Loss.* Grand Rapids, MI: Zondervan Publishing House, 1996.

Stanley, Charles. *How to Handle Adversity.* Nashville, TN: Oliver-Nelson Books, Thomas Nelson, Inc., 1989.

Tada, Joni Eareckson. *Glorious Intruder: God's Presence in Life's Chaos.* Portland, OR: Multnomah Press, 1989.

Taylor, Rick. *When Life Is Changed Forever: By the Death of Someone Near.* Eugene, OR: Harvest House Publishers, 1992.

Venden, Morris L. *The Answer Is Prayer.* Boise, ID: Pacific Press Publishing Association, 1988.

White, Mary A. *Harsh Grief, Gentle Hope.* Colorado Springs, CO: NavPress, 1995.

Wright, H. Norman. *Recovering from the Losses of Life.* Tarrytown, NY: Fleming H. Revell Company, 1991.

Yancey, Philip. *Disappointment with God.* Grand Rapids, MI: Zondervan Publishing House, 1988.

Yeagley, Larry. *Grief Recovery.* Keene, TX: Larry Yeagley, 1984.

Footnotes

Chapter 7: The Next Indicated Thing
   [1]Gerald L. Sittser, *A Grace Disguised*, 33.
   [2]Philip Yancey, *Disappointment with God*, 253.
   [3]Sittser, 102-103.

Chapter 8: The Real Questions
   [1]Lawrence J. Crabb, Jr., *Finding God*, 104-105.
   [2]Sittser, 114.
   [3]Yancey, 242-243.
   [4]*Ibid.*, 193.

Chapter 9: Our Benevolent—Butler?
   [1]Yancey, 209.

Chapter 10: A Matter of Expectations
   [1]James Dobson, *When God Doesn't Make Sense*, 146.
   [2]Crabb, 71.

Chapter 11: Where Are We When It Hurts?
   [1]Yancey, 201.
   [2]Viktor Frankl, *Man's Search for Meaning*, 93.
   [3]*Ibid.*, 86.

Chapter 12: The Necessity of Suffering
   [1]Ellen White, *The Ministry of Healing*, 472.
   [2]Elisabeth Elliot, *A Path Through Suffering*, 156-157.

Chapter 13: The Final Word
   [1]Yancey, 186.

Chapter 14: Preparing for Loss
   [1]Normal H. Wright, *Recovering from the Losses of Life*
      (quoting Richard Exley in *Rhythm of Life*), 132.
   [2]Larry Yeagley, *Grief Recovery*, 16.

Chapter 15: Helping Yourself in Loss
   [1]Yeagley, 31.
   [2]*Ibid.*, 32-33.

Chapter 17: Helping Children in Loss
   [1]*When a Loved One Dies...*, 22-24.

Epilogue:
   [1]Sittser, 42-43.
   [2]Max Lucado, *A Gentle Thunder*, 5-6.

For Additional Copies of this Book,
or Sandy's Album "Some Holy Morning"
Contact Your Local Christian Bookstore.

For Immediate Shipping
Using Visa/MasterCard, Call Toll-Free:

800-447-4332